BARKING PAST

This book is dedicated to my father's friend,
J G O'LEARY

First published 2002
by Historical Publications Ltd
32 Ellington Street, London N7 8PL
(Tel: 020 7607 1628)

© **Richard Tames** 2002

ISBN 0 948667 80 X
British Library Cataloguing-in-Publication Data
A catalogue record for this book is available from the British Library

Typeset in Palatino by Historical Publications
Reproduction by G & J Graphics, London EC2
Printed by Edelvives, Zaragoza, Spain

The Illustrations

Most of the illustrations come from the archives of the London Borough of Barking and Dagenham
at Valence House, Becontree Avenue. We would like to thank Mark Watson,
Acting Museum Curator, and his staff for their co-operation in making these available.

Other illustrations were kindly supplied as followed:
Aerofilms *171*
Roger Cline: *16, 131, 132, 136, 137, 138, 139, 144*
Essex County Record Office: *51, 56, 88, 111*
Guildhall Library, Corporation of London: *22, 35, 41, 43, 44, 47*
Historical Publications: *1, 6, 7, 8, 9, 11, 13, 15, 18, 23, 24, 25, 26, 27, 28, 29, 34, 36, 38, 40, 50,
53, 54, 55, 59, 63, 65, 91, 94, 100, 113, 114, 115, 140, 141, 166*
London Metropolitan Archives: *22*
Peter Jackson Collection: *85, 86*
Victoria County History: *31, 162*

BARKING PAST

Richard Tames

HISTORICAL PUBLICATIONS

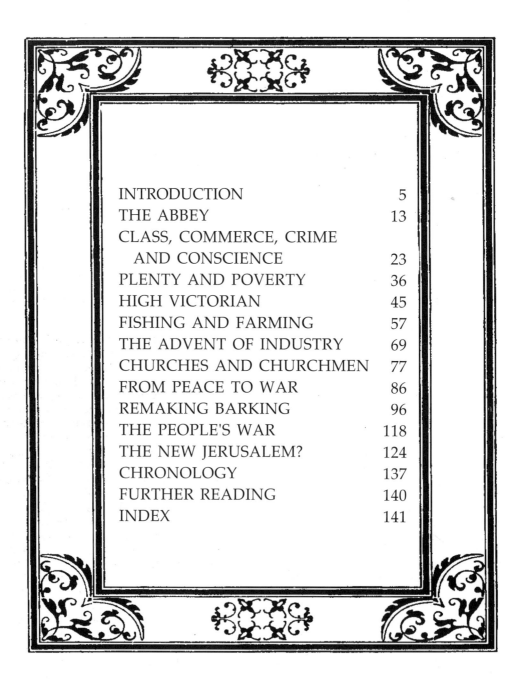

Introduction

" ... down at Greenwich, for slaves and tin,
The tall Phoenician ships stole in
And North Sea war-boats, painted and gay,
Flashed like dragon-flies, Erith way;
And Norseman and Negro and Gaul and Greek
Drank with the Britons in Barking Creek ... "

Rudyard Kipling: *The River's Tale* (1911)

"To the visitor, it appears to be just another suburb without well-defined boundaries ... Yet Barking people are conscious of its history as a town in its own right, one of the few real towns in present day outer London and therefore in some way different from the jumped up villages that surround it."

This view, implying some surprise at Barking's sense of communal identity and continuity with the past, was expressed forty years ago by two academic outsiders, investigating local government in the borough. London's self-styled biographer, Peter Ackroyd, writing in 2000, made much the same point, albeit somewhat brutally: "There is a harshness about Barking ... here a native population seems to have maintained its presence, with a kind of bleakness or hardness of attitude ... It remains a strangely isolated or self-communing neighbourhood, where the London accent seems peculiarly thick."

As if in belated agreement, Barking's borough council endorsed the importance of the locality's history in 2001 by adopting an official 'Heritage Strategy', which proclaimed that "The heritage is a largely untapped resource for people of the borough to enjoy, appreciate and to be proud of." The Strategy document further claimed that increased awareness of the local heritage would contribute to "pride in the community, educational achievement, local identity, cultural awareness and appreciation, community development and urban regeneration." A Jubilee visit by the reigning monarch to historic Eastbury House in May 2002 implied royal concurrence as well.

While recognising the self-evident significance of surviving historic properties such as Eastbury House and Valence House, Barking's Heritage Strategy accepted that the site of Barking Abbey had long been under-valued and that the creation of the vast Becontree estate, home to such a large proportion of the borough's residents, represented "a unique social experiment" of major impor-

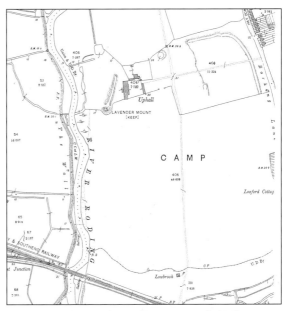

1. Portion of the Ordnance Survey map of 1894/6 showing the settlement site of Uphall and Lavender Mount.

tance in modern British history. One implication of this was a pressing need to build up an oral archive recording the impressions of those residents who could still recall the experience of the estate's early years. Oral history was also seen as particularly valuable for incorporating into the collective record the life experiences of those "lacking physical roots in the area".

Few communities in Britain can have had their own "physical roots" so profoundly transformed as Barking has over the course of the last century.

The most ancient site traditionally identified in the area was a trenched earthwork enclosing 48 acres around Uphall farm. The 1915 Ordnance Survey map still showed it as a residual line of earthworks and marked in Lavender Mount prominently. In 1964 it was still identified on the map reproduced in Volume V of the *Victoria County History of Essex* but it now survives only in the names of Uphall Road and Lavender Place. Victorian scholarly opinion was that this represented a British settlement subsequently occupied during the Roman period, with the mound, oddly placed on the rampart, as being possibly a much later Danish addition. Smart Lethieullier, lord of the manor of Barking in the early eighteenth century, believed that the foundation of one of Barking Abbey's great pillars was made of Roman brick and therefore thought that the Uphall

2. *Caesar at Uphall Camp, depicted in the Barking Historical Pageant of 1931.*

3. *A stone Roman coffin found on the site of 469 Ripple Road in 1932. It is thought to represent a pagan burial from the early 3rd century.*

remains were once a Roman town whose materials had been recycled to build and repair the abbey. By way of confirmation a coin of Magnentius was found on the site. Scattered Roman finds have since been made elsewhere. In 1876 E P L. Brock noted the presence of Roman flue tiles. Roman pottery was subsequently found on the site of the Lady Chapel. In 1932 the building of no. 469 Ripple Road yielded a stone coffin containing parts of several skeletons and a third century pot. The building of Westrow Drive in 1936 brought to light a brooch and Roman pots, including an unusual first century grey beaker, lying only eighteen inches under the surface.

Medieval Barking was the largest town in Essex after Colchester but only the extent of the Abbey's ruins and the generous proportions of the parish church now hint at this eminence. With a few exceptions, such as Loxford and Eastbury, even the names of most of the local estates, manor houses and mansions – Jenkins, Fulkes, Malmaynes, Bifrons – have quite disappeared from the map. Westbury, however, first mentioned in 1321 is remembered in the names of Westbury Road, the Westbury Arms of 1899 and Westbury school of 1904, now the Westbury Centre.

The oldest secular building in Barking town centre is now no. 35 East Street, a three-storey block, built 1822-60 and once known as Fawley House. The oldest pub site is occupied by the Bull at the junction of East Street and North Street.

Although the present building dates only from 1925 there are title deeds stretching back to the fifteenth century. Few ancient structures of quality remain. The only Grade I listed buildings are the parish church of St Margaret's and Eastbury House and its garden walls. The Curfew Tower and the Magistrates' Court in East Street are ranked as Grade II*. Grade II listing has been granted to the remains of Barking Abbey, the London Road bridge over the Roding, the Old Granary at the Town Quay, St Margaret's Vicarage and Barking station. Unlisted buildings of significance include the Fishing Smack pub of 1901 in Abbey Road, the 1931 Art Deco Burton's building in East Street, the Baptist Tabernacle of 1893 in Linton Road and the Town Hall. The Brewery Tap pub of 1894 is all that remains of Barking Brewery. Other unlisted but historic pubs include the Spotted Dog (1870), Royal Oak (1898), Red Lion (1899) and Jolly Fisherman (1906).

If relatively impoverished in terms of architecture, modern Barking can boast a goodly quota of local personalities who have achieved national eminence. Bobby Moore, captain of England's 1966 World Cup winning team, and his West Ham team-mate Trevor Brooking, were both born in Barking Hospital. Billy Bragg, the 'Bard of Barking', is not only Barking-born but the grandson of a Barking beer-house keeper. Other locally-born celebrities include pop idol Marc Bolan, Brian Poole, leader of the 1960s group, the

4. *The young Bobby Moore, captain of the Barking Primary Schools team which won the Crisp Shield in 1951.*

5. *George Carey, Archbishop of Canterbury.*

Tremeloes, and actor Ross Kemp – bad boy Grant Mitchell of the TV soap opera *Eastenders*.

Trinidadian Edric Connor, the first ever black member of the Royal Shakespeare Company, studied engineering at South East Essex Technical College. Comedian and TV personality Phil Jupitus dropped out of a local sixth-form college. Less well known, except among devotees of ice hockey is Jerry Davey. Born in Barking in 1914, he emigrated to Canada as a small boy but returned as a star of Britain's ice hockey team between 1932 and 1948, becoming its all-time greatest goal-scorer and the fourth person to be elected to the British Ice Hockey Hall of Fame. At the 1936 Berlin Olympics Davey came from his sick bed to give Britain a crucial goal over Canada to secure the gold medal.

Barking has also been the springboard for numerous distinguished careers in the church. Archbishop of Canterbury George Carey went to Bifrons School. Cardinal Heenan's first tenure as a priest was in Linton Road. Barking's vicarage has frequently been the stepping-stone to a bishopric.

Looking further back through the centuries, Barking can lay claim to an impressive line-up of historic personalities, as the following chapters will bear witness – the Good (Captain Cook), the Bad (Dick Turpin) and the conventionally successful – eight Lord Mayors of London. Local legend long held that Eastbury House was the meeting-place of the Gunpowder Plot conspirators on the grounds that they hoped to rendezvous there to watch the distant explosion of parliament to the west. Daniel Defoe repeated the story in the 1720s but modern scholarship brusquely dismissed the idea for simple lack of evidence. In 2001, however, local archivist Mark Watson revealed that at the time of the plot Eastbury House was not actually occupied by its owners, the Steward family, but sub-let to the Moores, who were Catholics and definitely related to a number of the conspirators - not conclusive proof but definitely intriguing.

From the medieval period Barking can claim St Erkenwald, founder of its Abbey, its re-founder St Dunstan and its temporary occupant, William the Conqueror. Adam de Barking (died 1216) was a learned monk and celebrated preacher at the Benedictine house at Sherborne, Dorsetshire. Richard of Barking (died 1246) became Abbot of Westminster, councillor to Henry III, Chief Baron of the Exchequer and Lord Treasurer of England and was buried in Westminster Abbey.

The first edition of Hakluyt's *Voyages* contains a narrative by a native of Barking, telling of a voyage to North America with Sir John Hawkins in 1582 and subsequent solo adventures in Mexico, from where he claimed to have travelled two thousand miles to be rescued from Cape Breton Island. It was omitted from later editions, quite

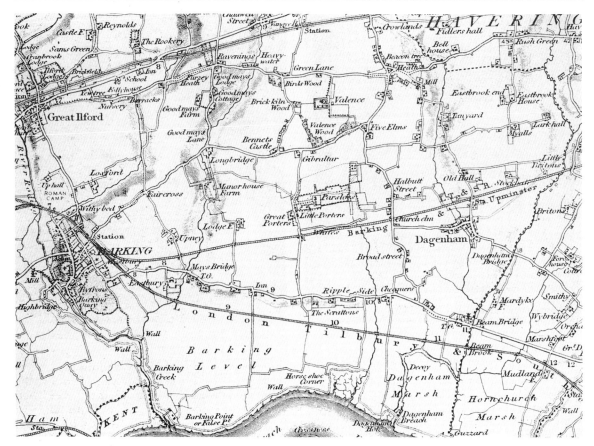

6. A section of the Ordnance Survey map for 1892 showing the still rural areas of Barking, Dagenham and Great Ilford, though now cut through by railway lines.

possibly on the grounds that, uncorroborated, it was too fantastical a tale to be true.

As a boy the philosopher and reformer Jeremy Bentham stayed at his paternal grandmother's house in Barking, which he found a positive paradise after the rigours of Westminster School and the confinement of a London home. Happy memories of childhood also haunted Mary Wollstonecraft, now remembered as both the author of the pioneering feminist tract *A Vindication of the Rights of Women* and as the mother of Mary Shelley, author of *Frankenstein*. As a young girl she lived with her feckless father in "a convenient house behind the town of Barking" for a couple of years. When she revisited it in 1796 to show it to her future husband, the radical William Godwin, she found the building untenanted and the garden overgrown.

James (*aka* Diego) Paroissien (1783-1827), born in Barking of Huguenot ancestry, grew up to study medicine. Embarking for Argentina in 1806, he became a significant figure in Latin America's struggle for independence from Spanish rule, serving as a field commander and surgeon-general with the forces of José de San Martin. One of the first persons to be honoured with naturalisation as an Argentine, he then played a leading role in the liberation of Chile and Peru.

In 1845 the Barking burial of Quaker prison reformer Elizabeth Fry drew a crowd of more than a thousand to pay their respects to a character and an achievement which had won her a European reputation and the admiration of princes. In 2002 posterity honoured her by printing her likeness on the five pound note.

Naturalist Alfred Russell Wallace (1823-1913) lived briefly in Holly Lodge, Tanner Street. Best known as Darwin's rival in formulating the theory of evolution, Wallace had been a convert to Spiritualism since 1866. Now remembered as a

7. Captain James Cook, from a painting by Nathaniel Dance.

8. Mary Wollstonecraft, from a painting by John Opie.

giant of Victorian science, he believed fervently in phrenology, opposed vaccination and was both a vegetarian and a socialist – though more in theory than in practice. Wallace certainly attended seances while living in Barking and may have held them at his own house, which acquired a reputation for being haunted. In 1871 "seized with a desire for country life" he moved on to Grays.

Barking became a separate parliamentary constituency in 1945 and each of its four representatives since then has achieved distinction, if of varying sorts. Its first MP was the Middlesex Hospital surgeon Dr. Somerville Hastings (1878-1967), who played a prominent part in the creation of Britain's National Health Service. President of the Socialist Medical Association from its foundation in 1930, he also served as a member of the London County Council from 1932 until its abolition in 1965. He was made a Freeman of the Borough in the year of his retirement from the Commons, 1959.

Although biographer Francis Wheen characterised Tom Driberg (1905-76), Barking's MP from 1959 to 1974, as the 'Soul of Indiscretion', he did manage to avoid outright scandal. A Communist activist at Oxford, sent down without a degree after a homosexual escapade, he launched himself on a career of constant self-reinvention, earning his livelihood variously as a pavement artist, gossip columnist, MI5 agent and war

correspondent, before finally finding a safe berth in Barking. In the 1920s Aleister Crowley, the self-styled 'wickedest man in the world', had singled out Driberg as his successor in this role. Instead Driberg contented himself with signing on with the KGB. Ennobled in 1975, Tom Driberg took his title from Maldon, where he lived in lordly style in a Georgian country house. He entitled his posthumous (1978) autobiography *Ruling Passions*. It mentions Barking just three times.

Driberg's successor was Josephine 'Jo' Richardson (1923-94), who served Barking until her death and was an ardent campaigner for nuclear disarmament and women's rights. A Memorial Fund was established in her memory in 2000 to assist women to enter higher education and in 2001 a new local school was named after her. Her successor, Margaret Hodge (1945) was appointed minister of state for post-school education in 2001.

Long-lived local families have, of course, been quite as important as outstanding individuals. Most eminent in the service of the state were the Fanshawes, whose portraits now adorn the walls of Valence House. Later came the Gascoignes and the Hulses. Over the past two centuries, however, few families have contributed as much to Barking as the Glennys who progressed from market gardening to farming, branching out into brew-

9.   Elizabeth Fry; watercolour by George Richmond.

ing and estate agency and finally emerging as a dynasty of civic leaders. Around 1815 William Glenny (176?-1850) took over part of the Bifrons estate which had been accumulated by John Bamber and dispersed by the Gascoignes. Edward Glenny (1800-81) built a new Bifrons mansion a hundred yards east of the site of the old one. Brewer Thomas Glenny (1842-1914) lived in The Paddock, an eighteenth-century mansion at the junction of Ripple Road and East Street.

Edward Henry Glenny (1852-1925) was the founder and secretary of the North Africa Nonconformist Mission, which had its headquarters in Linton Road. He also established Park Hall as a centre for the study and preaching of the gospel locally. Benjamin Wallis Glenny lived in the twelve-roomed White House, opposite which Thomas Glenny laid the foundation stone for a new Town Hall in 1893. In 1904 Westbury School was opened by retired farmer and Essex County Alderman William Wallis Glenny (1839-1923), first chairman of Barking Town School Board. Alexander Glenny (died 1935) was Clerk to the

Barking Charities, as his father, Samuel, had been before him and his auctioneer-estate agent son Kenneth (1900-1977) and grandson Keith were to be after him.

The public spiritedness of the Glennys has been complemented by the efforts of a distinguished lineage of self-appointed local chroniclers, stretching back to Smart Lethieullier. In the Victorian period land agent Edward Sage assiduously gathered materials for a history of Barking which progressed only to manuscript stage. He was followed by William Holmes Frogley (1855-1924), son of a Barking fisherman, whose reminiscences and sketches were subsequently acquired by self-taught antiquarian Fred Brand (1857-1939) and have recently at last begun to reach a wider readership through the editorial efforts of the current doyens of local historiography, Tony Clifford and Herbert Lockwood. Brand also compiled what became a standard bibliography on Essex history and in 1923 bought the Barking Abbey rental of 1456 at auction. He also developed an invaluable expertise in photographing early documents for his collaborator, Dr James Oxley (died 1994), who taught at Gascoigne School. The first Secretary of the Barking Archaeological Society and Editor of its *Transactions*, in 1935 Oxley produced a brief *History of Barking* and in the *Transactions* for 1936-7 a sixty page transcript of the Barking Abbey Rental of 1456. His 344-page study of *Barking Vestry Minutes and Other Parish Documents*, covering the history of the town's local government from the late seventeenth to the nineteenth century, was published in 1955. Dr Oxley also wrote the sections on Barking and Ilford for Volume V of the *Victoria County History of Essex*. From the Dagenham side of the picture honourable mention must be made of its charismatic and scholarly Chief Librarian, J G O'Leary (1900-85) and his longtime colleague James Howson (died 1993).

The fact that most of the script for the 1931 Charter pageant of the highlights of Barking's history was written by the ubiquitous Col. Loftus, headmaster of Barking Abbey School, rather than any of the above persons, may account for its selectively episodic depiction of the town's past. The nine scenes began with the Roman emperor Claudius at Uphall camp, followed by the foundation of Barking Abbey, the obsequies of Bishop Erkenwald (omitting the unseemly squabble over his corpse), the Viking sack of the abbey (enacted with frolicsome ferocity by Col. Loftus's own pupils), King Edgar's foundation of the second abbey, William the Conqueror at the abbey, the

10. *A sales notice of Edward Glenny & Son of 1931, depicting new shops and houses in Ripple Road and the Barking Park area. Notice the tie-in with the Pageant that year.*

11. *A class at Westbury School in Ripple Road, opened by Alderman Glenny in 1904.*

12. *John G. O'Leary, Chief Librarian of Dagenham and enthusiastic local historian of Barking and Dagenham.*

abbey at the height of its glory, the dissolution of the abbey, Elizabethan Barking, King Charles I playing a game of bowls at Barking and finally the Great Barking Fair as it was in 1746. Given the celebratory nature of the proceedings one can understand the omission of such dramatic but regrettable incidents as the execution of local witches, the burning of Barking's Protestant martyr, Hugh Lavercock at Stratford or the 1739 'Battle of Creekmouth' between local fishermen and the press gang seeking jolly jack tars to fight the Spanish. Given that the pageant was being mounted at the low-point of a world-wide depression, when the fear of unemployment hovered over every family, it might have been cheering to have reminded onlookers that in the recent past – totally ignored by the pageant-makers – Barking had been home to the world's largest commercial fishing fleet, the world's biggest jute factory and Britain's first aircraft factory and was currently home to both the world's greatest gas works, its biggest power station and its most ambitious public housing project. Future generations of local historians are unlikely to overlook the productive side of Barking's past in pursuit of the picturesque.

The Abbey

SAXON SAINTLINESS

The foundation of Barking Abbey is recorded by the Venerable Bede (673-735) in his *History of the English Church and People* as having occurred in 666:

> "At that time also when Sebbi ... ruled the East Saxons, Theodore appointed over them Earconwald to be their bishop ... before he was made bishop [he] built two goodly monasteries, one for himself, the other for his sister Ethelburga."

The foundation St Erkenwald (d. 686/693) established for himself was at Chertsey in Surrey. Erkenwald was of royal lineage and achieved such a reputation for holiness that after his death the very horse-litter in which he had been carried in his infirmity was credited with the performance of miracles.

Apparently a martyr to gout, he was subsequently invoked in prayer by fellow sufferers.

Tradition holds that Erkenwald died at Barking and that there then ensued an unseemly squabble for possession of his corpse between the canons of Chertsey and the nuns of Barking. (There is nothing inherently improbable about this part of the legend. The relics of a saint – and a royal one at that – were of such potential value to an institution in terms of its revenues and its reputation that considerations of propriety and even piety were likely to be overridden by those of property.) The canons emerged victorious, only to have their triumph thwarted *en route* to London by a sudden storm which raised the River Lea to dangerous levels. The equally rapid passing of the danger was interpreted as yet another miraculous intervention. Taking the hint, the canons decided to lay him to rest in St Paul's. This was doubly appropriate, not only because it was the seat of his diocese but also because he is credited with rebuilding it in stone after its first, wooden, incarnation had been destroyed by fire. Erkenwald's shrine became a great object of medieval veneration and pilgrimage until its desecration at the Reformation. His reputation for outstanding piety was such that, centuries after his death, it inspired an important poem in Middle English, recounting how (atypically) the corpse of a pagan (admittedly a conspicuously righteous one) resisted corruption until baptised

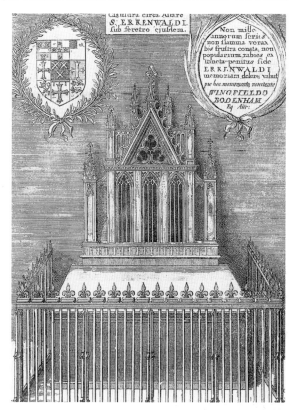

13. *The shrine of St Erkenwald, founder of Barking Abbey, at St Paul's Cathedral. The tomb was destroyed during the Reformation.*

by the saint's tears, but then "as sone as the soule was seysed in blisse", it instantly decayed. Less romantically the saint has also been commemorated in the names of a school, a church and playgroup, a Masonic Lodge and by the Barking and Dagenham Basketball Club, who compete as The Erks.

Bede recounts that the religious house at Barking was founded against the background of a devastating outbreak of plague, which, not unsurprisingly perhaps, caused many recent Christian converts to relapse to paganism. Ethelburga, nonetheless, persisted with the venture, undeterred – "she showed herself in every way worthy of her brother, in holiness of life and constant solicitude for those under her care". Bede further avers that at the time of her death (?676) a vision was seen, that when her body was brought into the church a miracle occurred and that she appeared to the mistress of novices, Saint Tortgith, curing her of a paralysis which had lasted six years. The chief value of all these various

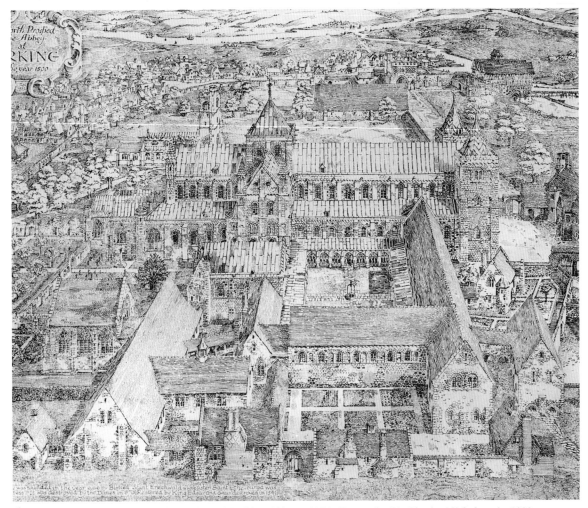

14. A reconstruction of the north prospect of Barking Abbey c.1500. Drawn by Sir Charles Nicholson in 1932.

traditions lies in the fact that Bede thought them worthy of record and that they provide striking illustration of the manner in which, for centuries before the papacy began to assert its monopoly on canonisation, sainthood was a matter of spontaneous attribution by the faithful.

Sebbi (?d. 695), king of the East Saxons, was an early benefactor of Barking Abbey. Unlike Sighere, his nephew and co-ruler, Sebbi remained a steadfast Christian throughout the testing times of the plague. Conspicuously pious, after a reign of thirty years he is said to have renounced his throne for the habit of a monk.

Like his protégé, Erkenwald, he was buried in St Paul's, where his supposed grave was shown until its destruction in the Great Fire of 1666, almost a millennium after his death.

The Abbey's earliest charter recorded the grant of land made by Hodilred, a kinsman of Sebbi c.692-3. The area seems to have lain between the River Roding and the Dagenham Beam River, as far south as the Thames. The northern boundary, less clearly defined, lay along the margin of the great forest of Essex. This land remained the core of the abbey's holdings until the Dissolution, thus constituting it as the oldest and one of the most enduring estates in the history of Essex.

Dedicated to the Virgin Mary, Barking followed the Benedictine rule and was destined to become the country's second largest religious foundation and the largest nunnery, occupying an eleven acre site, with an abbey church 330 feet long. It was England's first convent for women but was a double (though not mixed) community, in which

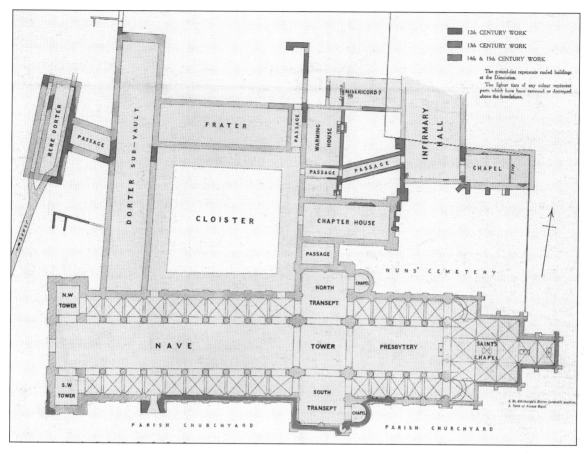

15. Plan of Barking Abbey, published in Transactions of the Essex Archaeological Society, 1913. *The darker shaded areas were thought to be 12th and 13th century.*

nuns and monks lived parallel lives of devotion. Although this was to become a not unusual arrangement at the time, it was disliked by Archbishop Theodore but it was left to Archbishop Dunstan, three centuries later, to ensure that the community would consist entirely of females, apart from the priest required to say mass and the laymen who did the physical work which maintained the institution and its inhabitants. Thanks to the presence of the abbey medieval Barking would become the largest town in Essex, after Colchester. The abbey's size and status was matched by the prestigious antecedents of many of its rulers. Ethelburga, the first abbess, was succeeded by Hildelitha "who had been sent for by the founder out of France, to instruct his sister Ethelburgh in the duties of her new station". She in turn was canonised and was followed by other abbesses of royal blood – Oswyth, daughter of Edifrith, King of Northumberland and

Ethelburgh, wife of Ina, King of the West Saxons. Cuthburgh, sister of Ina, who had been a nun under Hildelitha, founded the important nunnery at Wimborne, Dorset.

Apart from nuns who became saints, Barking was also credited by Bede with producing a child saint, Esica:

"who ... had been brought up and taught by these women vowed to God. Attacked by the plague and about to die, he three times called the name of one of Christ's virgins as though she were present, saying "Edith! Edith! Edith!".

Then he left this present world and passed to eternal life. The nun whose name he had called with his dying breath was at once stricken where she was by the same disease, and departed this life, following the child who had called her to the kingdom of heaven."

16. The north gate of Barking Abbey, published in The environs of London *by Daniel Lysons (1796)*

17. A Barking Abbey nun.

18. Seal on a Barking Abbey document.

DESTRUCTION AND REBIRTH

Although the offshore monastic settlement of Lindisfarne was raided by Vikings in 793, it was another forty years before they turned their attention to the south of England and not until 850 that the raiders over-wintered on Thanet. The incursion of a 'great raiding army' into East Anglia in 866 led to the foundation of a permanent Viking settlement at Jorvik (York) and the over-running of most of northern and eastern England by the invaders. Barking Abbey was sacked by Danes in about 870. This meant not only the massacre or dispersal of its inhabitants, the theft or destruction of its treasures and the firing and abandonment of its buildings but also the loss of control of the network of estates from which it drew its income.

The refoundation of the abbey a century after its extinction allegedly became intertwined with a saga of royal scandal and skullduggery. Edgar (dubbed 'the Peaceable' – i.e. his reign (959-75) coincided with a lull in Viking activity) – on visiting Wilton Abbey in Wiltshire, was smitten with the beauty of a novice there, Wulfhilda. Entreaties and gifts proving useless to entice her, he induced her aunt, Wenflaeda, Abbess of Wherwell, to feign illness and summon Wulfhilda to her bedside. The king, arriving ahead of her, seized the opportunity to press his suit with such fervour that she fled – so abruptly that the doubtless bemused monarch was left holding one of her sleeves. To protect herself from further advances Wulfhilda then took the veil, thereby apparently convincing Edgar of her piety and virtue. He apparently looked upon her henceforth as "a thing enskied and sainted", made her Abbess of Barking and endowed the foundation with rich estates. To this munificence she added twenty villages of her own while also herself founding a religious house at Horton. On Edgar's death, however, his widow, Queen Elfrida, out of retrospective jealousy, ejected Wulfhilda from both her houses – as Wulfhilda had once foretold she would. Wulfhilda was eventually restored to her position by Ethelred II (r. 978-1016), died at Barking and was subsequently canonised, the fifth abbess to be so honoured.

So much for medieval hagiography. What is certain is that Edgar was an enthusiastic supporter of the campaign of his mentor and close adviser, St Dunstan, bishop of London and subsequently Archbishop of Canterbury, to re-establish religious houses destroyed over the course of the previous century.

Although Edgar may well have been a benefactor to Barking, it had already been re-established before his accession because AD 950 is a definite date for the bequest of eight hides of land to the Abbey by his uncle and predecessor King Edred (r.946-55). Ethelred II, interestingly, named his own daughter Wulfhilda.

Excavations just outside the abbey precincts in 1996 revealed Saxon workshops, including a mill and a furnace where high quality glass was made *c*.900.

ENTER THE NORMANS

Following the submission of London to William the Conqueror and his coronation in the newly-completed Westminster Abbey on Christmas Day 1066 he chose to make Barking his personal residence and over the New Year 1066-7 he received the submission of the leading Saxon earls, Edwin of Mercia, Morcar of Northumbria, Edric the Wild, and Copsi, Earl of Northumberland. William also confirmed Barking's own holdings and privileges. Its abbess ranked before all others in the kingdom and was one of only four regarded as a baroness.

The manor of Barking, as recorded in the Domesday survey of 1086, was huge – thirty hides worked by seventy-one plough-teams. The land, which included Dagenham, was over twelve thousand acres. This does not include Ilford, for which there was a separate entry. About a third of the main manor, to the north, was forested. To the south was a broad band of marshland. Between lay the main cultivated area. The different types of land represented a good mix. The marsh would graze sheep and cattle and yield reeds for

19. Danes on the rampage in Barking, as depicted in the 1931 Barking Historical Pageant, using a cast of no doubt enthusiastic boys from Barking Abbey school.

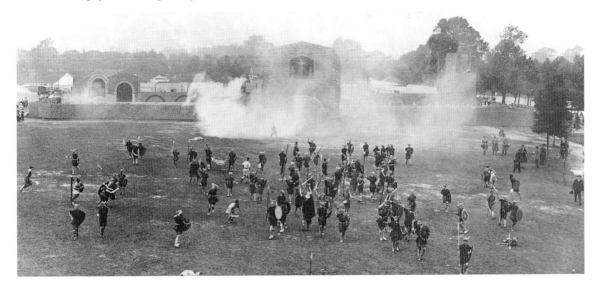

20. William the Conqueror, portrayed in the 1931
Historical Pageant by the vicar of Barking,

21. A stone cross found built into the wall of the Abbey.

baskets and matting. The forest would yield
acorns to feed pigs, as well as timber, nuts and
berries.

The manor's population was enumerated as
230 inhabitants plus six slaves. Allowing for wives
and children that might mean a total population
of up to a thousand. The livestock consisted of
two cobs, 34 cattle, 150 pigs (with woodland for
a thousand), 114 sheep and 24 goats. The other
resources of the manor included a fishery, two
mills and ten beehives. In London the manor held
28 houses, yielding 13s 8d and 'half a church' (All
Hallows by-the-Tower) in default of its rent of
6s 8d. The manor was valued at £80 in 1066 and
"now the same as the Englishmen state, but the
Frenchmen assess it at a hundred pounds." The
abbey either already held, or in due course was
to accumulate, many estates in Essex – at
Ingatestone, Great Warley, Tollesbury, Mucking,
Hockley, Horndon, Fobbing, Stifford, Bulphan,
North Benfleet, Great Parndon, Great Wigborough
and Abbess Roding. Holdings outside the county
included Tyburn and Stanwell in Middlesex,
Lidlington in Bedfordshire, Slapton in Bucking-
hamshire, Thames Ditton in Surrey and Fulbourn
in Cambridgeshire. In 1330 the Abbey acquired
as a gift a manor of nearly two hundred acres in

Dagenham known as Cockermouth, from its
donor, a Cumbrian priest in the household of the
bishop of Winchester.

Documentation survives from which the activities of two of the abbey farms, Westbury and
Dagenham (unidentified but near the marshes on
the Barking-Dagenham border), can be recon-
structed for the year 1321-2. Their pattern of
mixed farming balanced arable with livestock, at
least some of the latter being geared to market
demand. The biggest crops were oats (178 acres),
rye (112 acres), wheat (92 acres) and lenten barley
(76 acres). Beans (37 acres) and winter barley (5
acres) were also grown. These crops were reaped
by unpaid labour service. In the course of the year
the livestock handled included 700 sheep, 500
pigs, 800 chickens, 380 geese, 350 doves and 80
ducks. Most of the sheep were fattened on
marshland until ready for the London butchers
but over a hundred fleeces were also sold on.
Sheepskins would also have yielded the parch-
ment needed by a large, literate establishment for
its own records and documentation. Some ewes
were kept for milk, to be made into cheese. Twenty
ewes could yield enough milk to make 250 pounds
of cheese, a commodity much to be valued because it could be both sold and stored. The wisdom
of relying on a range of crops and livestock is
underlined by the fact that all the milking ewes
became diseased that year and had to be destroyed.

From its estates the Abbey derived produce

and services, many of which would, over time, be commuted for cash. A tenant at Warley was bound to do a turn as guard in the Abbess's prison. Another was bound to serve her as a carrier, taking messages or goods as far afield as Ely. A Dagenham tenant "paid 6s 6d yearly as rent and in addition had to ride with the Abbess round her manors once a year, or send a man, French or English, to do so." This latter form of service was required of some thirty tenants in the thirteenth century. One tenant was still performing this service as late as 1475. The detailed rental of Barking Abbey lands for the year 1456 reveals that a few tenants still owed harvesting services at that late date.

Another source of income was pilgrimage offerings. Barking's Holy Rood, dating from the twelfth century, or perhaps even earlier, once stood in the open and was believed to confer spiritual benefit on those who worshipped at it. It was subsequently moved into the Curfew Tower, where it survives, though much defaced. In 1400 the rood-loft chapel in the tower was licensed for the performance of divine services.

Royal patronage and involvement continued under the Normans, as it had under their Saxon predecessors. This relationship could cut both ways, leading to peremptory interventions in the

22. The Holy Rood at Barking Abbey, depicting the crucifixion. It is now housed in the Curfew Tower.

leadership of the community. Queen Maud, wife of Henry I, ruled as abbess for some years before her death in 1118. She is credited with the building of the first bridge and a causeway at Bow following an unpleasantly dangerous attempt to use the customary crossing over the Lea at Old Ford. For some years after 1136 the abbess was Maud, wife of King Stephen, then contesting the throne with Henry I's daughter, Matilda and doubtless reassured that his wife was safely ensconced in some comfort in a location which enabled her to guard his interests in turbulent London. Stephen not only restored to the abbey lands which Henry I had taken into the royal forest but also granted it the hundreds of Becontree and Barstable. A generation later in 1173, under Henry II (1154-89) the abbess was Mary, sister of the king's erstwhile favourite, Thomas Becket – doubtless an act of atonement for the martyrdom of her brother. Following her death in 1175, Henry appointed his own daughter, yet another Maud, in her place. In 1214 Pope Innocent III gave the Abbey the right to choose its own Abbess. In 1247 the daughter of King John – Maud – was elected.

Apart from the ruling house, the other main sources of recruitment for the post of Abbess were the daughters of the nobility of the Home Counties and of wealthy London merchant dynasties. In 1291-4 the Abbess was Isabel de Basinges, whose residence gave its name to Basing Lane in the City.

LITERARY LADIES

In the late twelfth century the abbey was home to an erudite nun called Clemence who translated into Anglo-Norman octosyllabic couplets a Latin biography of the fourth century St Catherine of Alexandria. The Latin original dates from c.AD1000 and the earliest extant manuscript of Clemence's *Vie de saint Catherine* from c.1200. In style it is similar to a life of Edward the Confessor, also written at Barking between 1163 and 1189, quite possibly also by Clemence. The Life of St Catherine is far from slavishly literal as Clemence felt free to embellish characterisations and omit passages which time had rendered irrelevant or incomprehensible to her intended readers. Clemence's evident sympathy for her aristocratic subject implies that she, too, came from such a background and her replication of the feisty saint's formidable debating skills implies a similar wit. Her writings have now become canonical texts for analysis by feminist literary academics.

Another, if minor, icon is Katherine de Sutton, abbess from 1358 to 1377. The *Newsletter of the British Theatre Guide* credits her with the invention of an Easter ceremony involving a religious play in the vernacular, including a 'Harrowing of Hell' sequence, aimed at and involving both the nuns and the local populace. Her innovation, if it was one, certainly built on an older tradition of Christmas dramas.

More prosaically, Sybil de Felton (abbess 1393-1419), who came from a prominent East Anglian family, arranged for the compilation of an *Ordinale*, setting out the Abbey's liturgical calendar and recording in detail the procedures to be followed on ceremonial occasions. The manuscript subsequently came into the hands of University College, Oxford and is now housed in the Bodleian Library.

NOBLESSE OBLIGE

The abbey's wealth enabled it to expand its own conventual buildings on a magnificent scale. The main church was probably rebuilt in the twelfth century and extended in the thirteenth to become 337 feet long, a length exceeded in Essex only by Waltham Abbey. The Fire Bell Gate, or Curfew Tower, is first mentioned in 1400.

Wealth also brought wider responsibilities. In 1145 Adelicia, abbess of Barking, founded a

hospital at Ilford, in effect as a retirement home for servants on Abbey lands who had become too old or feeble to work. This foundation later became a leper hospital. The abbey also established St Lawrence Spital for old women, in East Street, on a site later occupied by Wilde's almshouses. Between *c*.1180 and 1220 the abbey paid for the building in Kentish ragstone of Dagenham's parish church of St Peter and St Paul. Around 1400 a sanatorium was established out at Great Warley, where the abbey held one of the two manors into which that settlement was divided. Even abbey officials were wealthy enough to make bequests. William Pownsett, the last receiver-general of Barking Abbey, gave money for the repair of Loxford bridge and presented the advowson (the right to appoint the vicar) of Barking parish church to All Souls College, Oxford.

A RAP OVER THE KNUCKLES

Readers of Chaucer's *Prologue* to the *Canterbury Tales* will remember the bejewelled, fashion-conscious Prioress, devoted to her pets, obsessively refined in her manner and betrayed in her social origins by her Cocknified accent - the "frensshe of Stratford-atta-Bowe". Her priory stood at Bromley-Saint-Leonard, now completely obliterated by the A102 Blackwall Tunnel approach road, but in her day overlooking the Bow Bridge

23. The Curfew Tower at Barking.

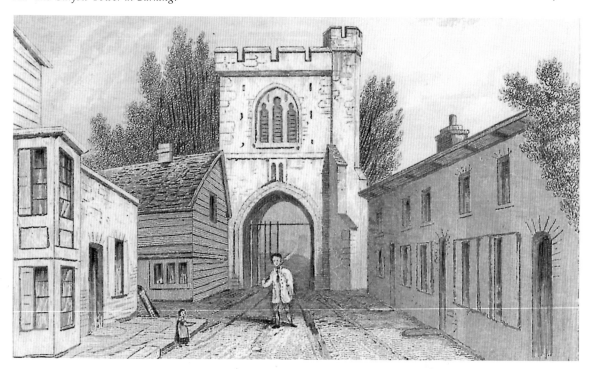

built by Henry I's Queen Maud. Chaucer's Prioress was a gently satirical portrait of a common enough type, probably the daughter of a wealthy City merchant who had opted out of marriage in favour of a comfortable life in a semi-rustic retreat but within easy reach of the little luxuries and gossip that London could provide. The fringes of a thriving commercial capital were never likely to become the natural setting for the practice of extreme religious austerities.

As of Bromley, so of Barking. A century before Chaucer, in 1279, Barking Abbey received a visitation from the bishop of London, followed by an official letter from Archbishop Peckham, confirming the bishop's strictures and adding further admonitions which reveal that more than a little slackness had crept into the Abbey's routines and observances. Henceforth celebration of the divine office should not be abbreviated. Nuns should be kept apart from other worshippers. The 'mystery play' performed on Holy Innocents' Day (28 December) should be staged by the nuns, not children, and not before outsiders "lest the praise of God be turned into a game". Silence should be more rigorously observed and evening chats in the parlour discontinued. All gates should be locked at sunset to prevent anyone from going out or coming in. No nun should speak alone to a man, except at confession. Nuns should only be allowed out only in the most exceptional circumstances, such as the imminent death of a parent "except which cause we can scarcely think of any grave enough." In any case they should never go out unescorted. Finally, it having been noted that some nuns showed a marked reluctance to perform unpleasant work, it was enjoined that the abbess should set them a personal example .....

A FINANCIAL WATERSHED

Despite its extensive property holdings, the Abbey's financial history was far from untroubled. Feudal rights were not always clearly defined. In 1187 the abbess was fined twenty marks for having 180 oaks felled "in the forest against the assize." In 1291 the abbess was licensed to sell timber from Hainault Forest to pay the costs of work needed in the marshes. Annual income at that date was just over three hundred pounds a year, a third of it from Barking itself. In 1302-3 Abbess Anne de Vedre was actually excommunicated for non-payment of papal tithes. In 1319 royal permission was granted to fell three hundred oaks to repair the abbey church and the

manor house at Loxfordbury after a fire.

A massive inundation at Dagenham in 1376/7 affected the Abbey's estates so badly it was reduced to 400 marks per year in income and it petitioned – successfully – for tax exemption. In the following year the abbess was excused muster duty, the costly assembly of an array of armed men for potential military service. In 1380 after great expense repairing the Thames dykes she was excused – in return for a small annual rent – a duty to maintain one and a half miles of fence around the royal hunting park at Havering. Further concessions were made in 1393. By 1409 the phenomenal sum of two thousand pounds had been spent on fruitless repairs to the banks of the Thames. (By way of comparison Henry V's entire Agincourt campaign of 1415 cost sixty thousand). In 1409 also, as though to damn all efforts at damming, six hundred acres of meadow were flooded at Dagenham and 120 acres of wheat elsewhere. Further financial concessions were made to the abbey throughout the fifteenth century. The catastrophe of 1376/7 inflicted damage which the abbey as an economic unit was never really able to make good.

ROYAL RESPONSIBILITIES

Royal connections brought another range of responsibilities in which the abbey served as a place of restraint, refuge or retirement. Elizabeth, wife of Robert the Bruce, was held prisoner in the precincts as surety for her husband's good behaviour from 1306 until she was transferred to closer confinement in Rochester as a precaution before Edward II's campaign into Scotland. The defeat of the English at Bannockburn in 1314 secured her release. In 1322 the powerful Despenser family, enjoying the favour of Edward II, had Eleanor de Burgh confined at Barking until she made over valuable possessions to them, though their extortion was subsequently reversed. Eleanor de Bohun, widow of Thomas of Woodstock, Duke of Gloucester, who had been kidnapped and murdered in Calais in 1397 on the orders of his nephew, Richard II, retired to the Abbey and died there in 1399. The brass on her tomb in Westminster Abbey depicted her as a nun of Barking.

From 1436 to 1440 Edmund Tudor (?1430-56), father of Henry VII, was kept at the abbey with his younger brother, Jasper, under the supervision of abbess Catherine de la Pole.

24. *The remains of Barking Abbey, with the tower of St Margaret's church in the background.*

DISSOLUTION AND DISAPPEARANCE

As the dissolution of the monasteries began with the smaller foundations Barking Abbey, with an annual income of just over a thousand pounds, was one of the last to go, being surrendered to the king's commissioners in November 1539. It had by then fallen to third wealthiest in the realm after Sion and Shaftesbury. Superior social connections, however, served it well to the very end. The last abbess, Dorothy Barley, was a friend of royal commissioner Sir William Petre, whose sister-in-law was one of the Barking nuns. The abbess was herself godmother to one of his daughters. She was granted a handsome annual pension of two hundred marks, with proportionately smaller sums to the thirty nuns. Demolition of the Abbey buildings began in June 1540 and went on for the following eighteen months. Much of the stone was recycled to build a royal residence at Dartford and lead from the roof was used for repairs at Greenwich Palace. The king's jewel house was enriched to the tune of 3,586 ounces of silver plate and a beryl-encrusted silver gilt monstrance. Selling off the livestock raised another £182 2s 10d.

The Abbey site and demesne (home) farm were subsequently granted by Edward VI to Edward Fynes, Lord Clinton who granted them the same day to Sir Richard Sackville. The Manor of Barking was kept by the Crown until 1628 when it was sold to Sir Thomas Fanshawe for two thousand pounds. In 1662 he left for the benefit of the poor the Market House and Tolls of Barking plus seven cottages and a stable. In 1754 the manorial rights were sold to the antiquarian Smart Letheiullier, who made the first attempt to excavate the abbey in 1724 and to sketch out its history. From him the manor passed to his niece, who married Edward Hulse Esq., in whose family line the rights passed until the extinction of manorial rights in 1926.

The north-east gate of the abbey was demolished in 1885. In 1911-12 excavations of the abbey precincts were made under the direction of Sir Alfred Clapham (1883-1950), later to become President of the Society of Antiquaries.

They failed, however, to unearth anything from the Saxon period but did expose the walls of the abbey church and cloister. Further excavations were made in 1966, 1971 and from 1984 onwards. Saxon remains finally unearthed in 1996 included the industrial facilities noted above and also carved bone, gold thread and jewellery, all confirmations of the abbey's affluence a millennium ago.

Class, Commerce, Crime and Conscience

A NEW ELITE

Barking was an attractive retreat for affluent Londoners even before the Dissolution. In 1532 Sir Robert Norwich (died 1535), Chief Justice of Common Pleas, was living at the Ripple Side manor of Parsloes, two and a half miles east of Barking Town. The Dissolution led to much former abbey land becoming available to London merchants and government officials with cash to inject into their newly acquired estates but also plenty to spare for display and charity. Samuel Stokes of Barking (died 1584) left to his wife his "lands and tenements" (note the plural) in the City of London, as well as goods and plate. The pick of his personal wardrobe went to a friend – "my sword and dagger, violet cloak, striped canvas doublet, buff venetians, a pair of nether stocks and a shirt." Forty shillings was left to Barking's church repair fund and an equal sum for the poor on the day of his burial, to be distributed in bread or money, plus another ten shillings for the bell-ringers.

Being so near London and so market-oriented in its agriculture, Essex was a highly permeable society in terms of inter-marriage with, and the disposal of estates to, outsiders. In 1560 the manor of Claybury was occupied by Sir Thomas White, founder of St. John's College, Oxford. In 1597 it housed Thomas Knyvett, who entertained Elizabeth I there. In 1652 the occupant was Thomas Fowke, a former Lord Mayor of London. There had been four other owners between Knyvett and Fowke.

THE POWNSETTS

William Pownsett of Loxford Hall developed a profitable business as a grazier, supplying the London market on a large scale, although this activity accounted for only a fraction of his fortune. At the time of his death in 1554 he had 520 sheep, valued at £78, all pastured in Barking, and was expecting another 176 beasts, valued at £268, bought at Birmingham fair the previous Michaelmas. Pownsett's total wealth was just short of £3,000, almost half of it in cash, and included a house in Eastcheap, one of the capital's major provision markets and hence a street much favoured by butchers.

Thomas Pownsett, probably William's nephew, styled himself 'Gentleman' but in 1590 left a will with some very ungentle provisions. All his lands went to his eldest son, William. His other four sons were each to get a £120 at twenty-one. One of his two daughters was left five pounds and childbed linen, plus five pounds for each of her sons. The other got nothing.

Pownsett's brother and sister were left a pound each. His eight servants were left sums ranging from eighty pence to forty pence. Three pounds was left towards "the new casting of one of the bells of Barking church." Nothing was left to the poor. William Pownsett, the favoured heir, died the following year – bequeathing an annual 13s 4d for distribution among the poor. The estate passed to his brother Henry, who lived until 1627. His son, William, sold Loxford and moved on in 1629.

THE SYSLEYS

Richard Sysley of Sevenoaks bought the manor of Eastbury. One of his younger sons, Clement (died 1578) was the probable builder of Eastbury House and a man seemingly determined to make a mark not only in his own time but on posterity. In 1560 he had laid out money in fees for a grant of arms. His new, imposing mansion was complemented by "barns, stables, orchards and gardens" and his lands were "fenced with pale and ditch". His other local holdings included a "Forest called my livery wood", a rabbit warren as well as "marsh grounds and meadows" and fifty acres of land which were both separately subleased. He also had half a dozen more distant holdings let out to other tenants. In addition to all this he held leases on Plumtree Marsh and on East Ham Hall and four other manors in the area around it.

In his will Sysley left money to his mother, Lady Allington, to his two brothers and to Peter and Edward Osburne, Aldermen of London, "to make a ring or some other jewel for a remembrance". To another 'brother' – possible half-brother? – Michael Flemming esquire, he willed the nominal sum of five marks. To a sister – not even named – "two kine, she to take her choice". To one male servant Sysley left twenty shillings a year for life,

25. *Eastbury House from the south-west, in 1798.*

26. *Eastbury House from the north-east, painting by John Buckler, 1823.*

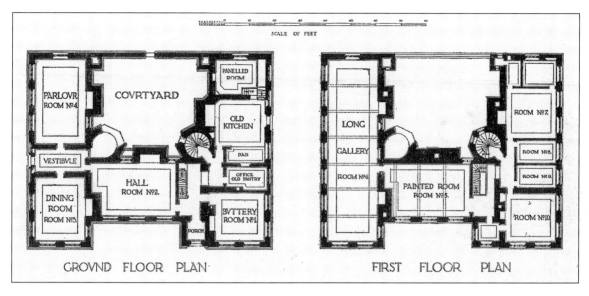

SCALE OF FEET

GROVND FLOOR PLAN·

FIRST FLOOR PLAN

27. Plan of Eastbury House.

to all the rest twenty shillings each. He left no bequests for the poor whatsoever.

Sysley's main heir was his eldest son, Thomas, who was specifically charged that his father's "armour and furniture, my guns, dags, pikes, bills, targets and crossbows ... are to remain as standards and implements of household to him and his heirs for ever at Eastbury". Sysley was clearly concerned about the destiny of this veritable armoury but failed to mention in his will any plate or other valuables. Doubtless his weaponry was valued less for its actual utility in warfare or the hunt than for its symbolic significance as evidence of gentle status and continuity with an appropriated martial past. Which was ironic in view of the way things turned out ....

Two years after Clement's death his widow, Anne, married Augustine Steward. Thomas Sysley turned out to be a wastrel, constantly dunning his stepfather for cash. Anne lived on for another thirty years, eventually selling her life interest in Eastbury to her son, also called Augustine Steward. He also acquired the reversion from Thomas of the property which was to remain "with him and his heirs for ever" but which in practice had passed out of the Sysley line within a single generation.

Another step-brother, who must have passed at least part of his youth at Eastbury, was the poet Thomas Campion (1567-1620), a step-son of the elder Augustine Steward from his first marriage. Campion and Sisley spent four years together as

28. The main entrance to Eastbury House.

29. *The Sysley coat-of-arms.*

30. *Frescoes at Eastbury House.*

fellow students at Peterhouse, Cambridge. Both left without a degree but Campion did at least start to study law subsequently before dropping out to serve abroad under the Earl of Essex. Campion later qualified as a doctor, published an argumentative treatise on poetic form and wrote masques for James I.

THE FANSHAWES

The Fanshawe family originated in Derbyshire and came to prominence, like so many others, through servicing the demands of the money-hungry Tudor regime. A younger son, Henry Fanshawe (1506-68) came to London to seek his fortune as a clerk in the Exchequer Office. By 1557 Henry Fanshawe was able to purchase the Barking manor of Jenkins. He also held Fulks in Barking, Valence in Dagenham and the leases of the Ilford leper hospital and its estate, Clay Hall, where he made his home. In 1566 he was appointed to the elevated rank of Remembrancer,

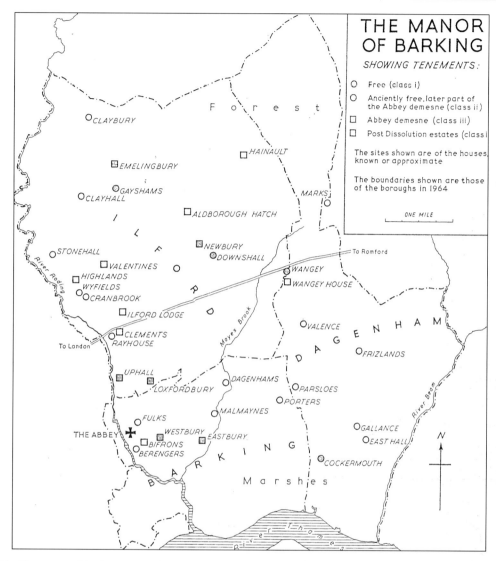

THE MANOR OF BARKING
SHOWING TENEMENTS :

○   Free (class i)

○   Anciently free, later part of the Abbey demesne (class ii)

□   Abbey demesne (class iii)

□   Post Dissolution estates (class i

The sites shown are of the houses, known or approximate

The boundaries shown are those of the boroughs in 1964

ONE MILE

31. *The manor of Barking. Reproduced from the Victoria County History of Essex, Volume V.*

a post which carried responsibility for taking care of tax records. Before his death he secured the reversion of his appointment to his nephew, Thomas (1533-1601), to whom he also bequeathed Jenkins, Fulks and the Ilford leases. Thomas chose to live at Jenkins. He sat in seven parliaments and composed a treatise on *The Practice of the Exchequer Court.* (Actually much of it was almost certainly drafted by his bureaucratic minions, with the title-page credit going to their chief.) The post of Remembrancer was to stay in Fanshawe hands for a century and a half.

In 1628 Sir Thomas Fanshawe (died 1631), eldest

son of the above Thomas, bought the manorial rights of Barking from the Crown for two thousand pounds. Compared to the eminence they had once enjoyed the later Fanshawes were crippled financially by their loyalty to the royalist cause during the civil wars. Yet in 1662 another Sir Thomas Fanshawe (died 1705) not only bequeathed for the benefit of the poor the Market House and Tolls of the town wharf previously noted but also seven cottages and a stable. A Fanshawe descendant, the Reverend Thomas L. Fanshawe was Vicar of Dagenham in the 1840s, representing three centuries of association be-

32.   Henry Fanshawe (1506-68).

33.   Thomas Fanshawe (1628-1705).

tween the family and the area. An outstanding collection of portraits of the Fanshawe family was collected together at Valence House by the indefatigable energy of Dagenham's Chief Librarian, J G O'Leary.

A GENEROUS BEQUEST

Sir James Cambell (1570-1642), who served as Lord Mayor of London and three times as Master of the Ironmongers' Company, accumulated a fabulous fortune but died childless. The many bequests in his will amounted to just short of fifty thousand pounds, including gifts to London hospitals, funds for the redemption of Turkish captives and £666 13s. 4d to found and maintain a free school to teach reading and writing to the children and youth of Barking. In a codicil he also left an additional hundred pounds to yield a rent charge of twenty pounds a year for the benefit of the school. "I know not whether it will please God to spare me life to accomplish my intention", Cambell declared in his last testament, requesting his executors to carry out his wishes in the event of his death. God did not spare Cambell

and it was left to his executors to erect the school and a master's house in North Street near the Bull Inn. It is clearly marked on the town map of 1653. No proper provision appears, however, to have been made for its repair and in the course of the following century the building became badly dilapidated so that it was pulled down to make way for the new workhouse in 1786-8. The rent-charge was then appropriated for parish use, a breach of trust which passed unchallenged and uncorrected.

Cambell's name is perpetuated in Cambell School in Langley Crescent.

GETTING AND SPENDING

The earliest reference to a market at Barking comes from the reign of Henry II, between 1175 and 1179. The first known reference to a shop dates from 1254. The market place, dominated by the market hall, remained the nucleus of the town. Variously known in its history as the Market House, Leet House, Court House and Old Town Hall, this imposing building was built in 1567-8. The locals levelled and paved the site and built twenty shopfronts and ancillary sheds to serve the market. The main construction costs of the actual building – the not inconsiderable sum of

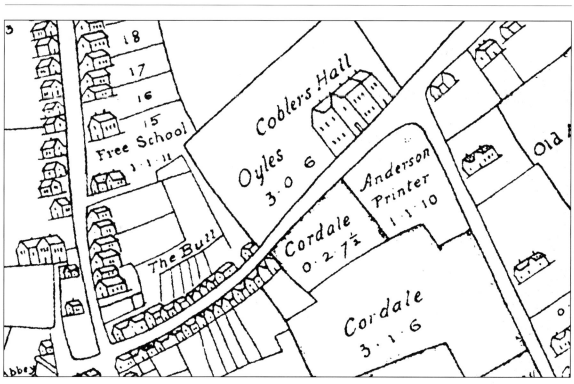

34. *Section of Thomas Fanshawe's map of 1653, showing the Free School founded by Sir James Cambell (1570-1642).*

35. *Barking Market House in 1799. Built in 1567-8, largely from funds supplied by Queen Elizabeth I, it was demolished in 1923.*

36.   *The Market House c.1912.*

37.   *The west side of the Market House, or Courthouse, in Back Lane, probably before the 1st World War.*

£324 – were borne by Elizabeth I, a notoriously parsimonious monarch but also lord of the manor and therefore with a vested interest in its prosperity. The accommodation consisted of a justice hall, where court sessions were held, and an adjacent room, with the comfort of a fireplace for magistrates' conferences. There was also a storeroom for the town armoury, another where the stocks were kept, a long, narrow schoolroom and a further small room, occupied by a poor man, who presumably served as watchman in return for his accommodation. Rents from the shops around the Court House helped to subsidize the poor rates. Over time, however, the magistrates began to favour the "comfort of hospitable inns", which doubtless offered the attractions of refreshment as well as a fireplace.

Barking's location at the confluence of the River Roding and an inlet of the Thames helped it develop as a point for loading and transhipment. In 1203 two ships taking bacon to Normandy are known to have loaded part of their cargo at Barking. In the fourteenth century the export of leather and wool are mentioned. The latter was produced on the abbey's own estates. In 1389-90 Nicholas Marchant of Barking was trading wool, via the port of Sandwich, with Holland. Timber, cut in Hainault Forest and intended for naval use, later became another important cargo to pass through the town quay. In 1737 the Roding Navigation Act was passed to improve navigation between Barking Mill and Ilford Bridge, mostly by dredging the river bottom and strengthening its banks, rather than more radical measures. The promoters of the Act argued that it would be "very convenient for the carriage of corn, coals and other food and merchandises to and from Great Ilford ... and to and from London and other parts, as likewise for the carriage of chalk and other manure...".

Hospitality towards travellers, especially ecclesiastical ones, was a duty incumbent on religious houses; but in the case of a nunnery this was often exercised indirectly, through the provision of an adjacent hostelry. Apart from helping to maintain the exclusiveness and serenity of a female establishment, it might well also prove to yield a useful source of revenue. A tavern certainly stood outside the abbey gate in 1456. By the seventeenth century, however, the names of Barking's taverns reflected its increasingly maritime character – The Dolphin, The Ship and The Blue Anchor. Local brewing to supply these premises is confirmed by leases referring to the

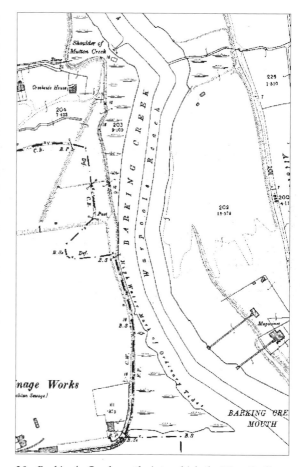

38. Barking's Creekmouth, into which the River Roding flows, shown on an 1894 OS map.

patch of land named Brewer's Croft (1626) and "a tenement called Old Brewhouse" (1641) occupied by Gabriel Salterly, brewer. Other local field-names in a lease of 1555 imply brick-making – "Brykfeld" and cloth-finishing - "Teintourcroft" and "Teynterfelde". (A tenterfield was one in which cloth was stretched.) A dyer is also known to have been in business in 1456.

With a plentiful supply of timber to the north, fine grazing marshlands to the south and a river to the west Barking was an obvious location to develop a tanning industry, which required plentiful supplies of bark, hides and water. A Barking resident called Odo the Tanner is mentioned in 1232-3 and in 1367 a boatload of hides is recorded as being brought downriver from London for tanning. Barking tanner Henry Noble is known to have been in debt to a London cordwainer (worker in fine leathers) in 1371. There are further references to tanners in 1369-74 and 1454-1461. The sole surviving medieval court roll of Barking manor, for the year 1440-41, contains a record of a fine for selling badly-tanned hides. The substantial scale of tanning at Barking is confirmed by fact that in 1520, when Henry VIII set out to meet Francis I in the tented city known as the Field of the Cloth of Gold, John Burr of Barking supplied him with 428 oxhides. Two London skinners held property in Barking in Tudor times. The name of Tanner Street preserves the memory of this once important local trade.

The extensive local marshes yielded osiers which were woven into baskets and hurdles, used to pen in grazing sheep. This may well have been a useful by-employment for slack times. A basket-maker is referred to in 1683. By the eighteenth century there would have been a steady demand for the bowl-shaped 'peds' used by fishermen to store their catch. There were still two local basket-makers as late as 1863.

The economic activities of Barking residents were not, of course, confined to Barking itself. In 1631 Nicholas Bingham, Gent. took out a 21-year lease on a chalk cliff and limekilns at West Thurrock at a hefty annual rental of £366 10s. Equally there is evidence of absentee ownership of Barking lands and houses by gentry residing in Romford and Stondon Massey.

CRIME

The haphazard nature of law enforcement until modern times leaves an equally haphazard imprint on the written record, that record's survival in turn being the product of chance and circumstance. Many incidents of petty theft and assault went unreported, either because there was little confidence that the unpaid (and often unwilling) constables and, also unpaid but usually more conscientious, magistrates, would or could do anything about them or because the aggrieved party had taken the matter into his own hands to achieve reparation or retribution.

Although the House of Correction for the whole of Becontree Hundred was located in Barking, by 1609 punishment of those who were caught and found guilty of crimes was as likely to involve fines or physical chastisement as periods of incarceration. Barking possessed both a pillory and a whipping post and stocks which were ordered to be repaired as late as 1831.

Barking's very proximity to London, the nation's largest centre of both professional and casual

39. Barking's stocks, as depicted in the 1931 Historical Pageant.

criminality, inevitably exposed its citizens to a degree of risk. In 1567 the house of Clement Sysley was raided by a gang of five Londoners armed with swords and pistols. They assaulted his five servants and, with the assistance of two London watermen, got away with spoons and a salt cellar worth six pounds and a further six pounds in cash. One of their number was identified as William Rogers, a 'gentleman,' and all seven were brought before a special Assize at Stratford within four days of the incident. Having confessed their crime, all seven were found guilty and hanged.

Unpremeditated violence was an ever-present threat in a town where so many men got their livelihood braving the dangers of the deep and rewarded themselves with bouts of binge-drinking. The example could be infectious. Edmund Fortescue Esq. reproved his servant for drunkenness, whereupon the servant ran at his master with a rapier, driving him into a ditch. Fortescue then drew his own rapier and thrust it into the servant's belly, causing a seven-inch wound, of which he died two days later. In 1581 a young man standing near the town's archery butts was fatally wounded by a careless bowman.

Occasionally a contemplated crime involved a high degree of imagination, even ambition. In 1567 John Segrave of Barking, mariner, was charged with counterfeiting the Great Seal of England attached to forged letters patent. He was found not guilty.

MISDEMEANOURS

Church courts dealt with matters that in a more secular age would be regarded as personal moral failings, rather than punishable offences against the social order. In 1564 Nicholas Weaver alias

Allsaundre confessed to incest with his niece, Dorothy. He was obliged to stand penitent for two days in Romford market, another day in Brentwood market, another in Barking market and on Sunday in Barking church. His wife was granted a judicial separation and half his property. In 1575 William Skott denied making his stepdaughter pregnant.

Bastardy was taken seriously, not just as a matter of sinful behaviour but because it had long-term economic consequences. The mother of a child born out of wedlock in a parish could claim support for it. There was, therefore, a very direct incentive to ensure that unmarried mothers were moved on before they delivered their offspring. In January 1586 Elizabeth Vaughan alias Jones was suspected to be in Edward Vaughan's home, pregnant but allegedly unmarried. James Vaughan, a gentleman, came forward to testify that he had been present at her marriage, two years previously, to one Robert Jones of St Katherine's, London, currently serving with the English expeditionary force in Flanders "under Mr. Philip Sidney in her Majesty's affairs." Vaughan's word seems to have been sufficient to restore the lady's honour. Oddly enough, however, an Elizabeth Vaughan was presented by the Walthamstow churchwardens in 1596 as having given birth locally but lacking a husband – whom she claimed to be a Mr Owen, serving on the Earl of Essex's expeditionary force against Cadiz.

In 1587 John Atkynson was accused of "having a suspected woman brought abed in his house and gone away unpunished." Atkynson averred that she was the lawful wife "of Christopher Wilson, one of her Majesty's Chamber", who had produced a marriage certificate from the Savoy chapel, which again proved sufficient to settle the matter.

WITCHCRAFT

As Essex produced more witchcraft accusations than any other English county it would seem unfeasible that a community the size of Barking would be entirely free of them. Their most interesting feature is the way in which they cluster together at particular periods. Accusations against Celia Glasenbery (1574), Joan Pynder (1576) Elizabeth Hardinge (1579 and 1580) occur in a decade marked by harvest dearths and are followed by a blank decade until a major outbreak of plague in London (1592) and a run of bad harvests (1592-5) coincides with accusations against Alice Foster (1592), Carter (1595) and Mrs. Jones (1596).

Celia Glasenbery, wife of a Barking yeoman, was accused of causing the deaths of three men and a grey gelding and the temporary paralysis of a fourth man. Tried and found guilty at Brentwood's brand new Assize House, she was sent back to Barking for her hanging. The incident was sufficiently high-profile to merit the publication of a pamphlet entitled *The Examination and confession of a notorious Witch named Mother Arnold, alias Whitecote, alias Glastonbury* ...

Elizabeth Harding was charged with bewitching to death Cecily, William Miles' three-year-old daughter, of causing great injury to Ellen, wife of John Goode, and of causing the death of twelve colts, valued at thirty pounds, belonging to Michael Towler. She was acquitted of the child's death but pronounced guilty of the other two charges and sentenced to a year's imprisonment at Colchester. When the charge regarding the child's death was revived against her at the assizes, halfway through her sentence, she was found guilty and hanged.

One suspects that accusations were more often made out of neighbourly malice than genuine fear, in the knowledge that the accused would, at the least be troubled and put to much inconvenience and expense. In the case of Alice Foster, for example, "suspected by common fame to be a witch", she was able to have her case summarily dismissed on production of a certificate of her innocence from the hands of Barking's churchwardens. But she still had to take the time and trouble of attending the archdeacon's court over at Romford and was obliged to pay sixteen pence in legal fees.

There are no more witchcraft accusations in Barking until, curiously, one final one against Martha Driver (1666) – just after London's last great plague and in the year of its Great Fire.

RELIGIOUS DIVISIONS

Barking was sufficiently near to the epicentre of political and spiritual conformity for religious observance to have been punctiliously enforced. Under Mary Tudor, Edmund Bonner, bishop of London, condemned Hugh Lavercock (or Laverick), a Barking man, to burn at Stratford in May 1556 with John Apprice (or Aprice) for clinging stubbornly to the Protestant faith. Lavercock, aged 68, was a former painter and a cripple. Aprice was blind. Their fate was illustrated in Foxe's *Book of Martyrs*. According to Foxe, when the aged cripple was secured to the stake by a chain he threw away his crutch and consoled his fellow martyr with the admonition "Be of good cheer my brother, for my lord of London is our good physician; he will heal us both shortly – thee of thy blindness and me of my lameness."

In 1559, when the religious pendulum had swung against the Old Faith, John Gregyll, Barking's long-serving (1524-60) vicar, was briefly imprisoned as a suspected papist.

Most backsliding was, however, minor in both its nature and its consequences. When one Haddon refused to accept Communion in 1564, because he objected to receiving it on the grounds - theological not medical – that the "priest had great pocks", he was fined two and sixpence nonetheless. In the same year a Mr Burre and his wife, known recusants, tried to excuse their absence from Easter communion on the grounds that "the plague was then in Barking town." It was, but they were still ordered to pay a shilling to the poor and to receive the sacrament within a fortnight. The assistant curate himself, John Horton, was arraigned before the archdeacon's court in 1579 as a "disquiet parson" and for "letting of children ... to be godfathers and godmothers, being not of sufficient age, contrary to the Queen's Injunctions." When Thomas Smythe was accused of failing to take communion at Easter in 1590 he could excuse himself merely by saying "there was such a multitude." In 1597 Jane Minors was in trouble for keeping her newborn infant unbaptized for a month, her excuse being "it was foul weather, I dwell three miles from the church" – and when she did at last come, she spent four hours in a nearby tavern first. In 1616 Thomas Cooper was charged with "morris dansinge upon the Saboth daye and drawing many idle and dissolute people to ale-houses at unseasonable tymes upon that saboth."

CIVIL WARS, UNCIVIL WORDS

Essex was firmly in the orbit of Parliament during the civil wars and puritanism was strong in the parish of Barking. At least two Barking men, James Daggs and William Parke, were among the first to enroll in the thousand-strong regiment of dragoons raised for Parliament in August 1643. The notorious radical John Lilburne became its colonel the following year. Barking's vicar, Richard Hall, judged insufficiently ardent in the anti-royalist cause, was effectively side-lined by the appointment of a succession of lecturers.

A Quaker meeting, one of the earliest, was formed in Barking around 1658.

In Barking, therefore, Royalists, especially outspoken ones, could expect to find themselves in trouble but this appears not to have deterred one particular termagant. In 1645 Robert White, a yeoman, was walking along Fisher Street when Margaret Edwards, a fisherman's wife, berated him as a 'Roundheaded Rogue' with such vehemence that he snatched a marsh fork (?for taking eels) from a marshman "to defend himself from hurt and violence". When Edward Palmer, a draper serving as parish constable, went to the Edwards' home to demand "some money due upon a rate, the same Margaret accused him of being one of a number who had "brought a Popish priest to town" and warned him menacingly that "the King is a-coming now and then we shall have a course taken with you and such as you are ...". When Margaret Edwards was brought before Quarter Sessions Nicholas Cleere additionally deposed that in the market place he had heard her denounce their preacher, Peter Witham, appointed by Parliament, as "a Papist dog".

A SNAPSHOT IN TIME

The earliest detailed map of Barking Town, made in 1653 for Thomas Fanshawe, provides a snapshot of the town's size. Four major roads with substantial ribbon development running along either side converge on the market place and surviving abbey gate-house. A north-south spine is represented by today's North Street and Broadway, terminating at what is now St Paul's Road to bear west and then south along the line of modern Abbey Road. East Street intersects this spine opposite the abbey gateway, with what will become Ripple Road running southwards from it. Almost all of the houses still have land around them or at least narrow burgage plots running away behind. All have views over open land or fields to their rear. Tomlins Orchard and a Bowling Alley add a rustic touch. Apart from the church, the mill and the free school the only building to be specifically identified is styled Coblers Hall . The holdings of substantial landowners are indicated by their names. Thomas Fanshawe himself holds a large central patch, Dovehouse Croft, just behind the houses on the east side of the market place, plus the Brick Field at the north-west corner of the town and another plot in the north-east quadrant, surrounded by holdings labelled Oyles, Norris and Barnes. The two largest holders are Oyles and, in the south of the town, Alderman Vyner, whose land spans both sides of the Roding. Other proprietors include Blotte, Bateman, Cordale, Gardiner, Mildmay, Anderson the Printer, M. Blackburne, Mr Clarke and Thomas Elliott – just over a dozen men in all.

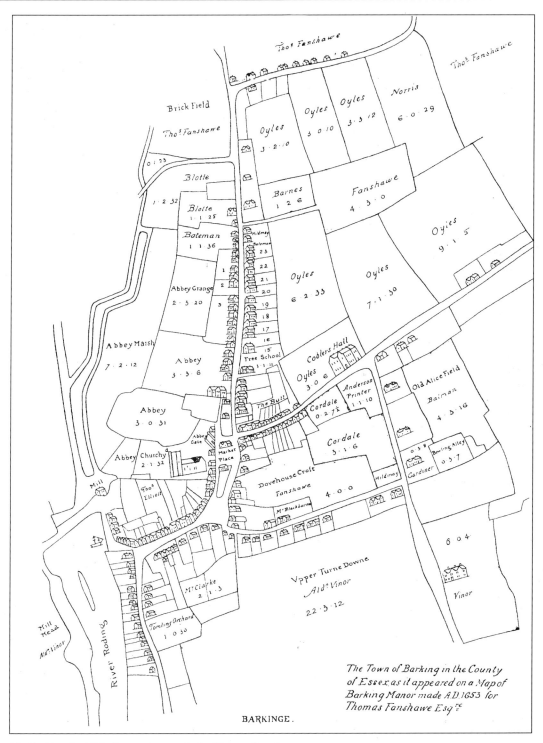

40. *Barking in 1653, from a map made for Thomas Fanshawe.*

Plenty and Poverty

Let Barking's ancient glory
Be told in song and story
In long and lasting lays
With hearts and voices joining
In gladsome songs combining
We sing her deathless praise.

With people in variety
We have a good society
To make us mortals blest:
In social love united
With harmony delighted
We emulate the best.

Our friendship and affinity
Surpasses consanguinity
As gold surpasses ore;
Success to every brother
Let's stand by one another
Till time shall be no more.

The Song of Barking 1730

Henry Carey's paean to social solidarity paints a prettier picture than the realities of life in Georgian Barking would justify. Although it had its share of the 'middling sort', local society also had its extremes – a select elite who lived in more than comfort and an underclass dependent on the public purse for mere existence. In the 1770s Barking had twelve shops and three butchers, which bespeaks a certain modest prosperity, but it also had a workhouse with 78 inmates.

The offspring of the local gentry had the option of attending a flourishing private academy kept by a Revd Mr Carter, one of many such on the fringe of the capital which enabled over-qualified and under-employed clergymen to supplement their incomes and live in a better or at least a larger house than they otherwise could afford. Their better pupils might be plausible aspirants to a university place or the learned professions. The rest were at least removed some distance from the temptations of the metropolis.

The labelling of Barking on Chapman and Andre's 1777 map of Essex betrays contemporary perceptions of the social as well as the physical landscape. The most prominent features to be picked out are Barking Mill, the 'Charter School', Tanner Street, Loxford Bridge and the major resi-

41. Westbury Hall c.1800.

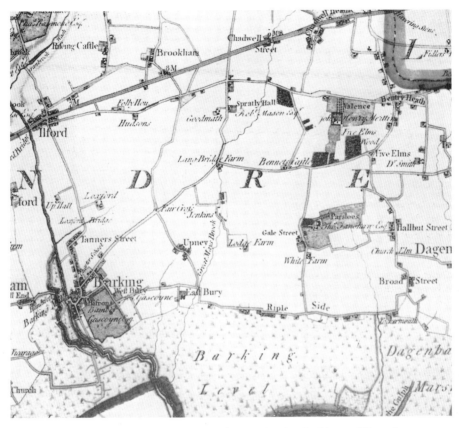

42. *Section of Chapman and Andre's map of 1777, showing Barking and Dagenham.*

dences of Bifrons, West Bury, East Bury, Loxford and Up Hall. Superimposed in flowing italic script are the names of Bamber Gascoyne Esq. and Jos. Gascoyne. At the southern end of Barking Level, safely distant from any significant habitation, is Barking Magazine. This was a government-owned gunpowder warehouse, established in 1719.

NEAR BUT FAR

It is difficult to imagine the perception and experience of distance in pre-railway England. Barking, though undeniably rural in its environs, was certainly thought of as conveniently near the capital. Many of Barking's inhabitants routinely walked into London and back again on business. Yet, as the location of the gunpowder magazine suggests, Creekmouth was regarded as safely remote from significant human habitation.

Longbridge Farm, on the road into Barking, was also sufficiently remote for its inhabitants to

be subjected to a harrowing ordeal on the evening of 19 December 1734. It had already been three hours since sunset when six armed men burst in on seventy-three year old Ambrose Skinner, who was alone in the farmhouse, apart from a young maidservant. The two of them were held hostage for the next three and half hours while the intruders ransacked the entire house, collecting a vast booty, ranging from silver and rings to clothes, wigs and bedlinen. While the robbers went calmly and systematically about their business, seemingly quite confident of being undisturbed, they also managed to capture two more servants and Skinner's son and wife as they returned home, all of which suggested that the intruders knew in advance what the movements of the various members of the Skinner household would be. Eventually they left with an estimated three hundred pounds worth of loot, half of it in cash, including two horses from the farm's stables, which they used to carry off their swag, riding

43. *Loxford Hall, c.1800.*

44. *View of Barking Market Place, 1804, with the Curfew Tower in the background.*

brazenly through Barking Town itself towards midnight.

Although the maidservant in due course gave evidence against the thieves, their unhurried proceedings suggest the possibility of her prior complicity – and subsequent betrayal? A number of the more valuable items stolen were later recovered by the Skinners from a receiver. The raid on Longbridge Farm was typical of a new and initially highly rewarding phase in the criminal career of one of the gang's members – ex-butcher Dick Turpin (1706-39). Having failed as a rustler and smuggler, he had turned to raiding isolated Essex farmhouses, terrorizing and, where resistance was encountered, torturing their inhabitants until they yielded their valuables. Turpin later graduated from highway robbery to passing himself off as a gentleman of means in Yorkshire until he was by chance apprehended for horse-stealing and the source of his 'means' was finally uncovered

GEORGIAN GENTRY

The Lethieullier family, originally from Brabant, built up holdings covering thousands of acres in Barking, Dagenham, West Ham, Chigwell and Theydon Bois, as well as other estates near London. Sir John Lethieullier (died 1718), sheriff of London in 1674, added Aldersbrook to the list. Smart Lethieullier (1701-60) was born at Aldersbrook House, the second son of John Lethieullier, son of Sir John, and Elizabeth, daughter of Sir Joseph Smart of Havering. After studying at Trinity College, Oxford Smart Lethieullier used the family fortune to further his antiquarian interests, travelling extensively in Europe, sketching and acquiring manuscripts, medals and marbles, some of which he housed in a small 'hermitage' he had built in the 'improved' grounds at Aldersbrook. His interest in local antiquities resulted in the first excavation of the ruins of Barking Abbey in 1724. He also wrote a history of Barking, a description of the Bayeux tapestry and an account of Roman finds at Leyton. On the death of his father in 1737 he inherited his estates and in 1754 purchased the Lordship of the Manor of Barking from Charles Gore. Lethieullier was one of the first donors to the British Museum and became a Fellow of both the Royal Society and the Society of Antiquaries. His drawings of Saxon and English antiquities came into the possession of the dilettante Horace Walpole. Lethieullier's collection of English fossils, displayed in two large cabinets, was described by the eminent

naturalist Peter Collinson as a "great collection, which excells most others." Smart Lethieullier chose to live and die where he had been born and was buried at Little Ilford in the family chapel. A few years later Aldersbrook was bought by Sir J T Long, who pulled down both house and hermitage.

Sir Crisp Gascoyne (1700-61) was born at Chiswick and set up as a brewer in Houndsditch. He settled in Barking in 1733 and his four youngest children were baptized there between then and 1738. Gascoyne played a prominent part in City affairs, serving as master of the Brewers' Company in 1746-7 and Sheriff of London and Middlesex in 1747-8. During the latter term of office he took the lead in persuading the Court of Common Council to take measures for the relief of orphans in the City of London. As Lord Mayor in 1752 Gascoyne became the first holder of the office to enjoy the splendours of the newly-built Mansion House. He was knighted in the year of his mayoralty and was also appointed a Verderer of Epping Forest. Gascoyne's wife, Margaret, was the daughter of a wealthy City physician, Dr John Bamber, who built the mansion of Bifrons in Barking. Margaret long predeceased her husband, dying in 1740 and being buried in Barking church, where Gascoyne himself was to be buried under a large monument, raised by his four surviving children.

The oldest of these offspring, named Bamber Gascoyne (1725-91) after his maternal grandfather, went to Felsted and then up to Queen's College, Oxford in 1743 and qualified as a barrister in 1750. In 1753, on the death of Dr Bamber, he inherited his property. Bamber Gascoyne served as MP for five different constituencies between 1761 and 1786 and was also Receiver-General of Customs and a Lord of the Admiralty. All of which makes him sound like a dull, driven careerist. But Gascoyne was also a prominent figure in county society, renowned as "a *bon vivant* and fond of good living", with a weakness for "waggery ". It was the custom on the first day of the Summer Assize to hold a Florist Feast in which the banquet of venison and turtle was accompanied by a prize flower show. Gascoyne once entered a cauliflower so immense that he demanded it be given prize of show: "the joke did not fail to amuse the party and to be long remembered as truly characteristic."

On the death of Bamber Gascoyne the Bamber estates passed to his son, also Bamber (1758-1824), who sat as MP for Liverpool (1780-96). The

45. *Bamber Gascoigne II (1758-1824), owner of Bifrons House, which he demolished c.1815.*

46. *Frances Gascoigne, daughter of Bamber Gascoigne (left), who married the 2nd Marquis of Salisbury.*

Bifrons estate comprised 221 acres around 1794 but had been reduced to 120 by 1809. Particulars of the mansion when it was offered for sale in the latter year note that it included an ornamental paddock of nearly eighty acres, the remainder subdivided into 'compact enclosures' and the whole 'enriched with stately timber'. In addition there were Pleasure Grounds with walks and shrubberies, a basin stocked with fish, a walled kitchen garden with fruit trees, a hot house, green house and ice house, stabling for sixteen horses and standing for five carriages. The main house, which had fifty windows, allegedly afforded, in an age delirious for 'prospects', "diversified Views of the adjacent Country, which is singularly rich and Picturesque, enlivened by the interesting Scenery of the Thames and bounded by the Kentish Hills". Alas, this idyll was doomed by Bamber Gascoigne II (1758-1824) to demolition around 1815. He then sold off both site and park to

William Glenny. Part of the estate was bought by Edward Glenny (died 1850) and after his death a new Bifrons mansion was built a hundred yards east of the site of the original. After Edward Glenny's death in 1881 this house was in turn demolished and what eventually became R White & Sons mineral water factory was built incorporating its materials. Bamber Gascoigne II's daughter and heiress married the second Marquis of Salisbury who added the named Gascoyne to that of Cecil, as well he might, given that the Bamber estates he acquired through his marriage were worth twelve thousand pounds a year.

Jenkins, a mile north of Eastbury, remained with the Fanshawes until 1717, when it was bought by London merchant Sir William Humphreys (died 1735). He replaced the ancient wooden house with a brick one and had gardens laid out with "terraces, vistas and avenues" and fishponds and a moat fed by the Mayes Brook. Smart Lethieullier

47. Bifrons House, a home of the Gascoigne family, in 1794. It was demolished in 1815.

bought the manor in the year of his death. Around 1768 Sir Edward Hulse demolished Humphreys' mansion and "worked up the materials into a good-sized farmhouse" known as Jenkins, later Manor, Farm.

A more ambitiously Arcadian project was contemplated at Claybury in 1791 when the celebrated garden-designer Humphry Repton prepared one of his famous Red Books for Claybury's owner, James Hatch. The Red Book offered the estate-owner contemplating the expense of major improvements a chance to envisage what he would be paying for in a series of before-and-after illustrations. Repton, who was based at Hare Street near Romford, viewed Claybury on 9 May and delivered his projected plans on 20 July. They depict views of artful rusticity with sheep, plantations of trees and a pleasure ground with a gravel walk. Repton's other major proposals for change were to destroy the existing hedges and install sunken fences and to change the entrance to the house from the south to the north side.

The outbreak of war against France in 1792 made such extravagances increasingly difficult to contemplate but Ripple Castle was built, with a mock-Gothic castellated frontage, at the junction of Lodge (formerly Castle) Road and Rippleside around 1800 and occupied by the Tyser

family. It still existed in 1938 and survived in the name of Castle Mixed School, now Castle Green Centre.

ALWAYS WITH YOU

For most of the eighteenth century the relief of poverty was the responsibility of the vestry. Apart from rates paid by local property-owners there was also an income arising from properties owned by the parish, most notably the town wharf and the market house and 24 shops conveyed in 1662 by Sir Thomas Fanshawe for the relief of the poor. There were also almshouses in East Street and a number of individual charities, providing for doles of cash or bread, usually funded by rents from land bequeathed by, or bought with, bequests from local testators. In accordance with the provisions of the 1697 Poor Relief Act paupers in receipt of parish payments were required to wear a badge identifying them as such. Between 1699 and 1722 the average number of Barking pensioners subjected to this humiliation was about sixty. A doctor was, however, contracted to tend them and occasionally they received gifts of clothing. Any who had children found that, from the age of eight or nine, they would be put out to an apprenticeship, whether the parents

48. The crenellated Ripple Castle on Ripple Road in 1920. Castle Green derives its name from this building.

assented or not. Under the terms of the same Act of 1697 tradesmen refusing to take on such children could be fined for their non-co-operation.

The poor rate for the parish as a whole (i.e. including Ilford and Chadwell Heath) rose from £521 in 1694 to £923 by 1714. In 1722 a workhouse was opened in four leasehold tenements in North Street. The usual motive for doing this was implied in its very name – a place where the poor would be obliged to contribute to their own upkeep by engaging in some form of productive labour. In 1734 it was decided that all those receiving relief should be obliged to enter the workhouse but the policy was not enforced rigorously and payments in cash and kind to out-pensioners continued. By the 1770s about fifty paupers were being accommodated in the workhouse, set to such tasks as winding silk, picking oakum and making mops. Meanwhile the poor rate reached £1,915 by 1772 and £2,058 by 1779.

In 1786 the Barking Workhouse Act transferred responsibility for relief from the vestry to a new body, the Directors of the Poor, consisting of the vicar, all resident JPs and six persons named in the Act. Vacancies thereafter were to be filled by co-option from parish property-holders rated at two hundred pounds a year or more or a life estate valued at a minimum of one hundred pounds. The directors, meeting at least quarterly, would be assisted by a treasurer, clerk and 'guardians of the poor', who would carry out their directions and 'overseers of the poor', who would continue to levy the poor rate and relieve the casual, rather than the long-term, poor. The directors were given control of all parish charities intended for the benefit of the poor in general, including Cambell's free school and the town wharf. They were also empowered to borrow

money or sell annuities, charged against the security of the rates. Funds thus raised were to be used to build a new workhouse. A resolution to this effect was the main business of the directors' very first meeting. Land was bought in North Street, adjoining Cambell's school and the work completed early in 1788. As one of the largest parish workhouses in Essex it was housing some 250 inmates by 1828. Initially they were set to making sacks and later to making cloth. As was typical of most such workhouse ventures these enterprises proved uneconomic and were eventually abandoned. In 1836, as a consequence of the national policy shift which created the harsh New Poor Law, responsibility for relief was transferred to Romford Poor Law Union. At the same time the expansion of Barking's fishing industry *(see pp 60-62)* created much-needed employment, diminishing the need for relief of the able-bodied. In 1841 Barking's workhouse was converted into half a dozen shops. Part of it later housed Barking's first public library before finally being demolished in 1936.

Renewed provision for the education of the children of the poor was made in 1810 when Cambell's defunct school was reorganised by a local committee which undertook to pay a master £15 a year and a mistress £10, to teach twenty boys and twenty girls. An additional five guineas was payable for teaching Sunday school. The children's clothing was also provided by the committee. By 1818 the number of pupils had greatly expanded to two hundred and in 1824 the school was merged with the National Society establishment. Boys were rehoused in 1827 in a new building in the workhouse garden, where Cambell's School had once stood, while girls and infants were accommodated in the old workhouse. Thanks largely to the efforts of Oliver Lodge, parish lecturer from 1809 to 1836, the number of local children receiving free education rose from just forty to some four hundred.

THE OUTCAST

Even less fortunate than the inmates of Barking's workhouse were those incarcerated in its House of Correction. Repaired and extended in 1686-8 and repaired again in 1718 and 1725, it was visited by prison reformer John Howard in 1776 and by the Essex magistrates in 1790. It was awful. The 'fore-gaol', for men, was just fifteen feet by ten feet six and the 'back-gaol', for women and children, even smaller – thirteeen and a half feet by eleven. Neither room had a chimney. Both had

49. The Workhouse in East Street, built in 1788 and demolished in 1936.

noisome sewers. There were no separate rooms for the sick or for inmates to work in. Hardened offenders, accused of major felonies, mixed with minor offenders. Because the yard was deemed insecure prisoners were often denied access to it and the pump it contained. Although there had only been a single prisoner, a misdemeanant, when John Howard inspected the premises in 1776, shortly before 1791 seven persons had been held there simultaneously. It was abandoned shortly thereafter in favour of a new building, intended to serve a wider area than Becontree Hundred alone, and erected in 1791-2 to the designs of the talented County Surveyor, John Johnson. Standing on a half-acre site, surrounded by a garden, it consisted of a separate house for the keeper, an infirmary and separate work-rooms and yards for men and women.

A pump gave 'excellent' water and inmates were set to picking oakum. In 1793 there were six prisoners, by 1806 fourteen. By 1819, when the disruptive impact of the ending of the Napoleonic wars had caused mass-unemployment and a discernible crime-wave, the number had risen to a staggering 120 and it was officially acknowledged that the premises had become overcrowded. Not until 1833, however, did Quarter Sessions finally decide to relocate the facility to a new building at Little Ilford. The Barking House of Correction was sold off the following year and demolished soon after.

FAIRLOP FAIR

"Let music sound as the boat goes round,

If we tumble on the ground, we'll be merry, I'll be bound;

We will booze it away, dull care we will defy,

And be happy on the first Friday in July."

A brighter side of eighteenth century life is represented by the emergence of an annual event which, even if it did not take place in Barking itself, almost certainly attracted a majority of its inhabitants and a century after its beginnings was still significant enough to command the interest of an artist of the stature of Thomas Rowlandson.

Daniel Day (1683-1767) was a Wapping businessman in the line of making blocks and pumps for ships. He also owned a small estate near Hainault Forest and on the first Friday in July was wont to combine collecting the midsummer rents due there with entertaining friends to a picnic of bacon and beans in the shade of the mighty Fairlop Oak. According to tradition the branches of the tree spread over an acre of ground and was "eight fathom round". The distinguished Swedish naturalist Peter Kalm measured it in 1748, putting its circumference as thirty feet and the spread of its branches as 116 feet. By about 1725 this annual sortie had become the nucleus of a substantial fair, with Day's entourage followed by a boat on wheels, bearing as passengers fellow-members

50. *The celebrated Fairlop Oak at fair time, portrayed by Samuel Hieronymus Grimm, 1774.*

of the block and pump trade and accompanied by a band. It was said that all the booths to entertain or sell things could be accommodated beneath the tree's great branches. The annual assemblage continued long after Day's death, he having been buried in Barking churchyard, appropriately in a coffin made from a limb of the Fairlop Oak.

In July 1810 the Spitalfields magistrate and prolific litterateur Joseph Moser contributed an 'Account of the Rise of Fairlop Fair' to the *European Magazine*. The Fairlop Oak itself was observed to be moribund by 1791, was damaged by fire in 1805 and blown down in a gale in 1820. In 1846 a 'Fairlop Fair Song', of which the chorus is quoted above, was printed in *Ancient Poems, Ballads, and Songs of the Peasantry of England*, published by the Percy Society. Editor J H Dixon characterized the fair at that date as "one of the gayest of the numerous saturnalia kept by the good citizens of London. The venerable oak has

disappeared, but the song is nevertheless sung and the curious custom of riding through the fair, seated in boats, still continues to be observed." In that same year PC George Hall was fatally injured by being thrown from his horse "after fifteen hours on duty at Fairlop Fair." A decade or so after this, following the passage of the 1852 Disafforesting Act, which allotted the entire area to the Crown, the government had the traditional site of the fair enclosed to shut out the public. Undeterred, the public relocated opposite the Old Maypole at Barkingside, then opposite the Bald Hind at Chigwell and then back opposite the Old Maypole. It is claimed that in 1863 the fair was still attracting over 100,000 people, which seems a huge number. Although the fair was still being held in 1900 it appears to have lapsed shortly afterwards. A new Fairlop Oak was planted near the pub of that name to mark the 1951 Festival of Britain.

High Victorian

Britain's first national census, taken in 1801, showed the population of Barking to be still little more than that of a large village – 1,585 in the Town Ward plus 280 in Ripple Ward. Although population numbers rose steadily over the following decades this constant increase was confined to an area little larger than that depicted on the map made for Thomas Fanshawe in 1653. The expansion of the fishing industry created new jobs but the incomes thus created were converted into slums rather than urban expansion as families crammed into existing properties. Perhaps the fact that fishermen were away so much of the time made the overcrowding more tolerable. One exception was Union Terrace, a neatly uniform row built in 1826 and "occupied by a very respectable class of fishermen."

The census of 1841 recorded the population of Barking Town itself as 3,751, while Ripple Ward's 467 inhabitants lived in 91 houses, scattered over the marshes extending down to the river. In fact the figure for Barking was extremely misleading because when the 1841 census was actually taken some 980 fishermen and their apprentices were absent at sea and so the true population was around five thousand. In that same year Bark-

ing's streets began to be lit by gas. The first police station was built in North Street the following year.

In White's *History, Gazetteer and Directory of Essex* (1848) Barking is characterized as "an improving town and fishing port ... greatly improved during the last eight years, by the erection of many new houses and shops and the formation of several new streets. It is now well paved and lighted". It was also noted that the Elizabethan town hall was still used for public lectures, "dances, penny readings and other social events" and for sessions of the ancient court leet which still met to deal with environmental offences involving blocked ditches or stray animals. White's upbeat impression of the locality is contradicted by clear evidence of overcrowding in 1851 when Barking Town had over 10% more families than houses. The investigative journalist Henry Mayhew was informed in the 1850s that there were four taverns in Barking whose main source of income was providing overnight accommodation for tramps, estimated at between forty and fifty in number.

Mid-Victorian society, far from being full-bloodedly bourgeois, was still sufficiently feudal for White's to list the district's major landowners – the Earl of Mornington, the Marquis of Salisbury, J S Thompson Esq., the trustees of the late R W H Dare, B de Beauvoir and B Bond. There

51. Union Terrace in 1900. According to William Frogley, from whose manuscript and drawings this illustration is taken, it was built in 1826 and was afterwards the residence of 'Captains of the Fishing smacks'.

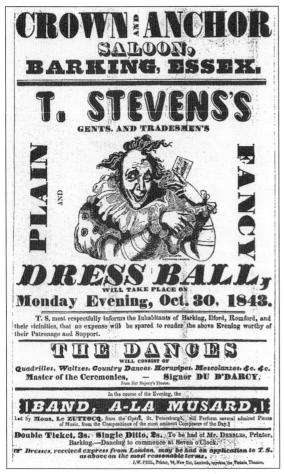

52. Advertisement for entertainment at the Crown and Anchor, 1843. The location in Barking is unknown.

was also a reverence for heritage, revealed in the recording of the names of the medieval estates and manor houses of the area – Jenkins, Loxford, Fulkys, Porters, Eastbury, Westbury, Gayschams Hall, Uphall, Stone Hall, Clay Hall, Great Geries, Aldborough Hatch, Bifrons and Highlands.

Local religious institutions were listed as the parish church of St Margaret's, a Wesleyan chapel and a Baptist chapel, the Quaker meeting house having fallen into disuse. Local affluence was evidenced by the existence of a Savings Bank with seven hundred depositors, whose combined wealth exceeded eighteen thousand pounds.

Barking's professional elite consisted of three surgeons, a registrar who doubled as assistant overseer of the poor, three clergy and the organist of the parish church, four insurance agents and an actuary, a surveyor/auctioneer, a doctor, a solicitor, a police sergeant and five 'gentlemen'. As in so many still semi-rural areas on the fringe of London there were six private academies, four of them run by females. Of the proprietors of Barking's nine inns and taverns two of whom were women, one was also a coach proprietor. Another of the publicans managed the gas works. The dozen or so retailers of a century previously had greatly expanded. Unsurprisingly the food and drink sector was the largest – 25 grocers (four female), 14 beer-sellers, 11 each of bakers (three female) and butchers, half a dozen greengrocers, a brewer and a fish salesman. Given the importance of fishing to Barking the existence of just a single fishmonger is only odd at first glance. Most people had much more direct ways of getting fish than from a shop – from a family member, a neighbour or a friend. There were also still three graziers to supply livestock to local or London retailers. Building provided employment for seven carpenters and builders, three each of painters and plumbers and two timber merchants. Keeping up appearances provided a livelihood for sixteen boot and shoe makers, nine tailors, four milliners and a hatter. Other retailers included seven drapers, three chemists, three coal merchants, two booksellers/stationers, a toy and hardware dealer and an ironmonger. Barking craftsmen included two braziers and tinners, two coopers, a pipe maker and a cabinet maker. The still slender service sector consisted of five hairdessers, all men, and three daily carriers to London. There were also buses to London at 9.30 and 5 and four postal collections daily.

The opening of the London, Tilbury & Southend Railway in 1854 hastened the pace of change, as did the building of the Victoria Dock in 1855, which created a new source of employment. Although the population level rose a little during the 1850s growth resumed in the following decade, despite the local collapse and re-location of the fishing industry. Population expansion at last began to be matched by the expansion of the built-up area. By 1862 in the north of the town King's Road, Queen's Road and Linton (originally Station) Road had been laid out to the west of the railway and Church Road and Bamford Road (then Bamford Place) to the east. Most building consisted of terraces of small houses or cottages with a few detached or semi-detached dwellings.

Urban expansion was matched by institutional growth. In 1851 a Barking branch of the Foresters' Friendly Society was established. By the 1860s

53. *One of the platforms of Barking Station at the beginning of the 20th century. At that time the railway bisected the line of East Street and Longbridge Road, requiring the installation of a level crossing.*

54. *Another view of the level crossing at Barking Station early in the 20th century.*

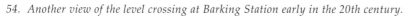

55. *The route of the railway also demanded level crossings at Ripple Road (above) and Tanner Street. The crossing at Ripple Road was replaced by a bridge only in modern times.*

there was also a Mutual Improvement Society which had a library and organized entertainments. An Amicable Association served as a forum for local tradesmen seeking to promote the general improvement of the town. For many it was not improving fast enough. The Local Board of Health, which had first met in 1853, had been dissolved by 1855, although there was a Barking and East Ham Provident Dispensary in Heath Street by 1863. In 1867 Roden Lodge was burned down in the middle of the night. It took two hours for a fire engine to arrive from Stratford because it had been "previously engaged at a fire at Bromley." A local newspaper noted scathingly that "it is a disgrace to the inhabitants of Barking that they have not an engine, with hose &c in proper order ready for immediate use, in case of being required, and not to have to depend on engines belonging to other parishes"– not to mention the lack of a proper water supply. The mains of the South Essex Waterworks Company finally reached Barking in 1873 and in the same year the Vestry at least discussed the question of purchasing its own firefighting hoses.

A telegraph service, portent of modernity, became available in 1870. In 1872 a new building for the Church of England National School was put up in Back Lane at a charge of £4000. It had to be enlarged in 1875.

BARKING FAIR

The suppression of Barking Fair in 1875 represented a distinct break with one of the vestiges of rural tradition. Held on the festival days of St Ethelburga, 22-24 October, it had taken over most of the centre of the town. In mid-Victorian times the townspeople spent freely at sideshows and shooting galleries, treated their wives to donkey rides and their children to gingerbread and gingernut biscuits. Pubs erected dancing booths in their rear gardens. The Fredericks family put up a travelling theatre opposite the George Inn and Wombwell's famous menagerie occupied a site by the horse-pond adjoining the old Abbey wall. In 1875, however, the leaders of several Barking congregations combined to get up a successful petition to the Home Secretary, despite the campaign led by auctioneer Jimmy Holmes who took space in the *Essex Times* to voice his opposition *(see illustration 56)*. Holmes complained that he would like to know:

ESSEX TIMES
13 Mar. 1875

BARKING FAIR.

ANNOUNCEMENT OF SALE.

MR. J. HOLMES

WILL hold his NINTH ANNUAL SALE, at Barking, on Friday, October 22nd, 1875 (in commemoration of Lord Holland, who departed this life October 22nd, 1840), for the SALE of LIVE & DEAD STOCK, and returns his sincere thanks to his numerous Friends and Patrons for the support he has received; and he also wishes to know if any of his supporters have a wish to Abolish the Annual Fair, which he has enjoyed over 50 years. If they have not he hopes they will sign the Petition for its continuance. He also would like to know by whom, or on whose authority, they have dared to attempt to abolish that which has given so much pleasure to the real inhabitants, born in the Town—thorough breds—not those who have come among us without being invited, many of whom think they are somebody, but in the opinion of the "Old uns" are considered Jack Straws, and in some cases a nuisance. My consent has never been asked, and any person or persons so committing themselves for the future will have notice to quit.
                                    JAMES HOLMES.
N.B.—Those who wish to reply must sign their names.
The Petition lies at the George Inn for Signature. It has to be sent to the Secretary of State, on Monday next. All respectable persons are invited to sign it, and any person professing that which they do not possess, wishing to sign, will be shewn the shortest way out.
                    By order of the Celebrated Jimmy.

56. James Holmes' broadside in the Essex Times protesting against the closure of Barking Fair.

"... by whom, or on whose authority, they have dared to attempt to abolish that which has given so much pleasure to the real inhabitants, born in the Town – thorough breds – not those who have come among us without being invited, many of whom think they are somebody, but in the opinion of the 'Old uns' are considered Jack Straws".

THE END OF THE CENTURY

A map of Barking as it was in 1875, immediately prior to an explosive growth in its population, shows that the station and railway track marked in effect the eastern boundary of the built-up area. A passenger arriving at the station and turning left would within minutes have found himself walking along the present Longbridge Road through market gardens past Faircross Farm, opposite where Faircross School now stands. North-west of the station, however, the first streets of Barking New Town had been built, although the ground north of Tanner Street was still open fields and there was nothing between

the western end of Tanner Street and the River Roding.

In 1883 historian Edward Walford described Eastbury House as "a large dreary, tumble-down mansion ". He was scarcely more complimentary about the town itself ... "it is straggling and irregular in plan ... The streets are poor, narrow, squalid and badly drained." But he also noted that the thirty parishes which comprised the rural deanery of Barking had nearly doubled in population since 1871. Many of the newcomers, he observed sniffily were "clerks and workmen who have been forced out of London by the reduction of cheap house accommodation; and the publicans are often almost the only people in the parish who keep a domestic servant."

As well as Londoners moving out there were Essex folk moving in. By the 1890s Barking and Ilford were joined to East Ham by unbroken lines of building. Barking New Town, now extended to the area east of the railway, consisted of streets of uniform two-storey terrace houses, slightly larger than the cottages of the early railway age, with small front and back gardens symbolising the social aspirations of their Pooterish white collar occupants. To the south of the town the streets between Fisher Street and King Edward's Road seem to have been intended for industrial workers, rather than clerical ones. The Broadway and Linton Road were "kerbed and metalled" in 1885. In 1887 Church Road was "sewered and made up". Union Street was "made up, sewered and kerbed" in 1889.

The residue of the former Bifrons estate was built over by 1895.

NEW FACILITIES

The growth of Barking's population from 16,848 in 1881 to 25,214 in 1891 to 62,781 by 1901 was at last parallelled by improvements in infrastructure and innovations in institutions. Barking Local Board, established in 1882, and largely superseding the vestry, immediately inaugurated a sewerage scheme for the Town Ward at a cost of £21,000. Indeed there was much catching up to be done. The inauspicious origins of Barking's hospital provision can be traced to an isolation tent hastily erected to cope with an outbreak of infectious diseases in 1885. An Infectious Diseases Hospital opened at Upney Meadow in 1893, which later became Upney Hospital.

A Burial Board for Barking was established in 1884 and Rippleside Cemetery opened in 1886. In the same year a volunteer fire brigade is known

57. James Holmes, who protested against the closure of Barking Fair (see illustration 56), was licensee of the George Inn at the junction of Axe Street and Broadway. When the Fair was abolished in 1875 he continued to give away ginger-bread to his customers on the fair days. Holmes died in 1881. The site of the George is now taken by the Captain Cook pub, built in 1961.

58. Faircross Farm in 1898. Faircross School was built on its site.

to have been in existence. In 1888 Ilford and Chadwell Wards became detached from Barking to form the new civil parish of Ilford. Barking station was rebuilt in 1889 and in the same year an Industrial Cooperative Society opened in North Street.

A School Board, established in 1889, opened Gascoigne school for 1,409 children in Howard Road in 1891 and Northbury and Barking Castle School, Rippleside in 1897. The Roman Catholic School was rebuilt in 1889 and enlarged in 1902. The impact of this new provision was to hasten the closure of older facilities. The Wesleyan school, opened in 1845, reached a peak attendance of 336 in 1887 but declined rapidly thereafter to 140 in 1899 and closed shortly afterwards. Other closures included the Church of England School at Creekmouth, the Congregational School in the Broadway and Rippleside National School.

In 1893 the Board took over the town wharf and in 1894 a water tower was built.

In 1893-4 an imposing new Town Hall, to the

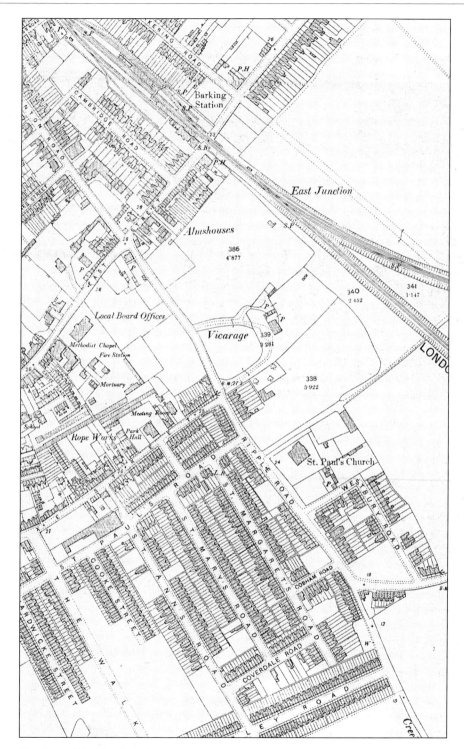

59. *Central Barking in 1894.*

60. *A dilapidated Eastbury House in 1894.*

61. *Barking Broadway in 1880.*

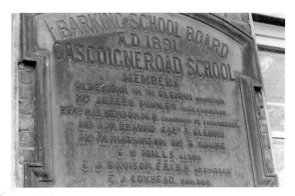

64. *A stone plaque on the wall of Gascoigne Road School.*

62. *The chapel at Rippleside Cemetery in the 1890s. Until the introduction of all-figure telephone numbers in London, Barking undertakers appropriately had the use of the RIPpleway telephone exchange.*

63. *Barking had a volunteer fire brigade by 1886, but by the end of the century fire fighting was under the aegis of the Metropolitan Fire Brigade, which had begun operations in 1866. The Barking Metropolitan Brigade is pictured below in 1925.*

designs of C J Dawson FRIBA, was built in East Street on the site of a former market garden. The foundation stone was laid by Thomas Wallis Glenny and the opening ceremony performed by the publisher-philanthropist J Passmore Edwards. The building contained not only council offices but also a library, fire-station, mortuary, stabling and sheds. The total cost was just over £15,000.

Barking Urban District Council met for the first time in 1895 and immediately sought powers to

65. *The old Barking Town Hall in East Street, built in 1894. It is now a magistrates' court.*

66. *A group of men, in 1894, who replenished the oil in public lighting. They used hand carts to carry the drums.*

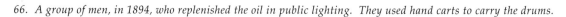

67. *Barking Council meeting in the baths in East Street in 1936. During the winter the baths were covered over and the area used for meetings, concerts and dances.*

68. *Barking Town Football Club in 1926.*

69. A local amateur team, Curfew FC, in 1910.

provide an electricity supply and a tramway service. It also launched a slum-clearance programme. In 1897 Barking UDC took over the powers of the burial board and bought a steam fire-engine. In 1898 Barking Park was opened and in 1898-9 a new swimming baths and laundry was built next to the fire station in East Street. Electricity supply to private houses became available in 1899.

SPORTING DAYS

As a visibly new Barking came into being sport provided a focus of loyalty and identity for its inhabitants, helping to integrate native-born and newcomer. There was a Barking Quoit and Skittle Club, which met at the Peto Arms. Beckton cricket club was founded in 1878, drawing its entire team from the gas works' employees. By 1907, with a membership of seventy, it was regarded as one of the strongest in the county, including in its ranks

men who had played regularly for Essex and Kent.

Football increased greatly in popularity following the establishment of the Essex County Football Association by eight clubs in 1882. By 1905 the ECFA had a membership of over 243 clubs. Barking Rovers FC had been founded in 1880. Vicarage Field football ground was opened in 1884 with a match against Ilford, the current holders of the Essex senior cup. Barking won 2-0. In 1889 Barking Rovers moved to Eastbury Field following accusations that they had damaged the cricket pitch. Vicarage Field was taken over by Woodville, from Forest Gate. In the 1895-6 season Thames Ironworks, precursor of West Ham United, needed three games to win a cup tie against Barking Woodville. After winning the South Essex League Woodville disbanded in 1900 to be replaced by the recently formed Barking Working Lads Institute team.

Fishing and Farming

A ROUGH TRADE

The earliest reference to salt-water fishing by Barking men dates from 1320, followed by other references in 1349 and 1406. All three relate to reprimands for using nets with too fine a mesh, contrary to law and to the detriment of the long-term viability of the fishery. During the incident in 1406 Alexander Boner, the official charged with enforcing the conservation regulations, seized sixteen offending nets only to be pursued by a mob firing arrows at him. He entrusted the nets to local constables but the nets were 'rescued' by their owners the following day. Some of the fishermen were later arrested, tried and found guilty but they were pardoned on condition of presenting their nets at Guildhall for approval. In the reign of Henry IV (1399-1413) Barking men were also charged with piracy.

A MAJOR EMPLOYER

The Barking Abbey Rental of 1456 makes several references to a 'Fisshamles' – i.e. Fish Shambles – which implies that the sale of fish was by that date sufficiently important to have a part of the market area specifically devoted to it. In the same document a William Fulk is described as a "fissher". A reference dated 1574 states boldly that "all that inhabit there are fishermen", which was certainly an exaggeration. Eight Barking fishermen did, however, contract with Elizabeth I's Comptroller of the Navy to supply fish to the fleet during Lent. Another document, from the reign of Charles I (1625-49), lists twenty vessels sailing out of Barking, each with a crew of four. Although the repair of boats can be dated back to the reign of Henry VIII, the first that can definitely be dated as built at Barking were the *Nonsuch* and *Endeavour* of 1655.

In 1631 Barking fishermen protested that they had obeyed a new government decree not to use a trawl net but that the men of Mersea and Burnham had not.

Repeatedly throughout the seventeenth century Barking men were accused of taking oysters from the rivers Crouch and Roach, contrary to the Earl of Sussex's monopoly. Others are known to have sailed as far away as Ireland.

FOR THOSE IN PERIL

The case of John Anderson in 1646 shows that even European waters offered hazards almost unimaginable to their families at home. Anderson was sailing across the Bay of Biscay in a London-bound ship when it was seized by Turkish pirates and he was sold into slavery. Anderson's distraught father petitioned Quarter Sessions for assistance in raising the astronomic sum of eighty pounds demanded for his ransom. In doing so he was hoping not for a donation but a licence "to ask, receive and take the charitable benevolence of godly disposed people within this County of Essex whose hearts God shall move towards the redeeming of this distressed captive."

In 1703 John Fryer was taken by the press gang to serve under Sir Cloudesly Shovell against the French and "had his back, his left arm and his thigh broken with the wind of a cannon ball". Being therefore "utterly disabled to work" to support his family, in 1708 Fryer petitioned Quarter Sessions "to take into consideration his most deplorable condition and allow him an annual pension to be paid him quarterly out of the county stock of charitable money." At least Fryer got back to his family. Admiral Shovell, having taken Gibraltar, sailed home in triumph only to make a massive navigational error which wrecked his fleet off the Scilly Isles. The admiral, possibly commemorated in the Ripple Road public house, the Ship and Shovel, made it to shore only to be murdered by a local woman for his emerald ring.

A certain amount of smuggling as a by-trade can be assumed. In 1630 Barking fishermen petitioned against royal officials extorting fees when taking bonds against smuggling excisable goods. Their complaint was vindicated to the extent that they were granted the right thereafter to seal their bonds before local JP Sir Thomas Fanshawe of Parsloes. But, even if fishermen were regarded as potential lawbreakers by the authorities, in time of war they were glad enough to press Barking men into the navy or to use their boats as fleet auxiliaries. At the time of the second Jacobite rising in 1745, when a French invasion was imminently expected, twenty to thirty Barking ships were placed on alert. In 1739 and again in 1803 local resistance to the press-gang was so general and so violent as to merit the name of riot.

A KNOWLEDGEABLE OBSERVER

Daniel Defoe, passing through Barking in 1722 in the course of collecting material for his *Tour through the Whole Island of Great Britain*, characterized it as "a large market-town, but chiefly inhabited by fishermen, whose smacks ride in the Thames, at the mouth of their river, from whence their fish is sent up to London to the market at Billingsgate, by small boats ...". He also noted that they regularly sailed to fish the coast between Shoebury and the mouth of the Colne, taking mainly sole "sometimes exceedingly large and yield a very good price at London Market" but also turbot, whiting, codling and flounders.

Defoe was also aware that more than economics was involved:

> "these fishing-smacks are very useful vessels to the public on many occasions; as, particularly, in time of war, they are used as press-smacks, running to all the Northern and Western coasts to pick up seamen to man the navy when any expedition is at hand that requires a sudden equipment. At other times, being excellent sailors, they are tenders to particular Men of war; and, on an expedition, they are made use of as Machines for the blowing up of fortified ports and havens...".

A document of the 1720s lists fourteen Barking smacks, each crewed by a master and four men. In 1800 a smack-owner named Tyler testified before an enquiry on the state of fisheries that he alone employed forty sail and had eighteen more building. Lysons, topographer of London's suburbs, in 1811 put the Barking fleet at seventy strong. In 1832 it was recorded that the town had 140 large vessels, crewed by five to six hundred men.

CAPITAL CONSUMPTION

Barking's position as the nation's biggest single fishing port was assured by its proximity to the enormous market London represented. In the right conditions smacks could sail right up to Billingsgate itself, offering London dealers the chance to buy the freshest catch available to them. At worst the capital was a brisk cart ride away. Fishing ports which would become important in the future, such as Grimsby or Brixham, had as

70. Fishing smacks at Barking in the 1860s.

71. *Barking Town Quay in 1832.*

72. *Frescoes depicting the local fishing industry in Eastbury House.*

73. *Scrimgeour Hewett (1769-1850).*

74. *Samuel Hewett ((1797-1871).*

yet only a small and relatively impoverished hinterland to sell into and, before the coming of railways, no means of reaching big inland cities while the catch was still fresh.

Barking had, moreover, other natural advantages than its location. The Creek was navigable for vessels up to 400 tons and after 1737 was navigable to Ilford for boats up to 80 tons. Barking also offered the facilities of a natural dry dock where a vessel grounded on sloping banks at high tide could have its bottom scraped and repainted in twelve hours or less. The smacks themselves could also be built locally.

THE SHORT BLUE

During the nineteenth century Barking was to be dominated by the Short Blue fleet created by Scrymgeour Hewett (1769-1850). A Fifeshire man, he had initially come down to Dagenham to look after an aunt's property and then in 1794 married Sarah Whennell, daughter of the owner of two smacks. Hewett went into business with his father-in-law, retaining the square blue house flag flown on the mast of his smacks but greatly enlarging their number. Nevertheless, in deference to his senior partner, he insisted that the Short Blue,

which was to become in its time the largest single commercial fishing fleet in the world, dated not from their partnership but from 1764, when the first boat had been acquired. During the Napoleonic wars Scrimgeour obtained letters of marque and sailed as a privateer. Returning home, he found that his second son Samuel (1797-1871) had himself run away to sea. Taking him on as his own apprentice, Scrymgeour gave his son his first command at the age of nineteen, appropriately called *Liberty's Increase* and soon turned the effective direction of the business over to him. His confidence was not misplaced. By the time of Scrymgeour's death his fleet had grown to 220 ships, crewed by 1,370 men and boys. Of the latter many were orphans, recruited from the Foundling Hospital in Bloomsbury. Apprentices made up half the crew on most smacks, which must have kept costs down.

White's Essex *Gazetteer* of 1848 commented approvingly that "The fishery is the nursery of a hardy and industrious race, who seldom fail to become excellent sailors." It listed 75 masters of ships. There were four Harrises, three each of Baxter, Marchent and Gale and two each of the Butterfield, Chalk, Cotterill, Earl, Forge, Morgan,

75. *Barking Creek frozen over in 1895.*

76. *A ship of the Short Blue Fleet in 1864.*

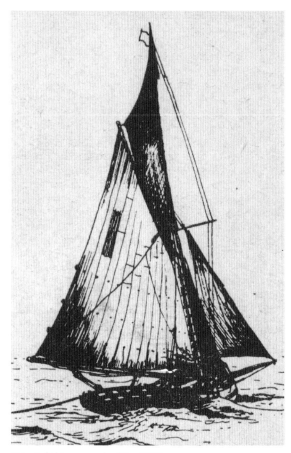

77. A fishing smack of the 1860s.

Shelitoe and Sunaway families. Many other occupations at that date were directly related to the fishery. There were six sail-makers, five mast, pump and block makers, five shipwrights and boat builders and four rope and line makers. In addition to this there were four marine store dealers, four slopsellers and two ship chandlers, as well as makers of specialized products such as ship's biscuit, sea-boots, kegs, casks and nets. A former inhabitant reminisced "how fragrant Heath Street and Fisher Street smelt of tar and pitch, how well the stores were supplied with sou'westers, oikskins, big-boots, guernseys, red caps, hawsers, ropes and twine."

By the time Hewett and Whennell went into partnership it was already an established practice for the farmers of the Barking area to allow their low-lying lands to flood in winter to make ice. Harvesting this in winter and carting it off to storage afforded welcome employment to many who might otherwise have had little or no farm or building work during severe weather. Samuel Hewett systematised the business and around 1846 built two large ice-houses with walls thick enough to keep the thousands of tons of ice right through summer. He also set up Britain's first artificial ice-making plant but this proved too expensive and the experiment proved abortive.

In 1837 a fishing ground for sole, known as the Great Silver Pits, was discovered out in the North Sea. Its potential seemed limitless and the London market offered an equally limitless source of demand. The problem was getting the catch there fast enough from so far north. Samuel Hewett also realised that holding the catch in the traditional 'peds' – round-ended wicker baskets – was not best calculated to optimise the carrying capacity of a boat. He also fretted that smacks returning to Barking to unload or make repairs were using time that could have been more profitably spent catching more fish.

Hewett therefore organised his fleet into two classes of vessel. One type stayed on station for four to eight weeks, catching fish, the other acted as a carrier, plying backwards and forwards between fleet and market, carrying the catch, pre-packed by the catching crews, in square boxes, which were stacked in tiers in their holds, with a layer of ice between each tier. Carriers sailed out with fresh provisions for the catching crews plus eighteen tons of ice on board and returned with forty tons of fish layered between it. Meanwhile Hewett developed a ship-repairing base at Gorleston on the Norfolk coast, which was a hundred and twenty miles nearer the fishing-grounds. This was not only a thriving fishing community in its own right but, more important, offered space for further expansion of support services.

END OF AN ERA

In 1862 Samuel Hewett relocated his fleet head-quarters to Gorleston. The following year Barking's remaining fishing community suffered a terrible blow when sixty fishermen were lost in a gale off the Dutch coast. In 1865 the railway reached Great Yarmouth, beyond Gorleston. The existence of fast, cheap rail links to London and the ability to buy ice cheaply from Norway effectively nullified Barking's previous locational advantages. Many Barking families followed the Short Blue to Suffolk and by the time of the 1881 census Barking-born people accounted for an eighth of the population of Gorleston. Other Barking families moved up to Grimsby and developed the industry there. Only three smack owners were listed in Barking in 1870.

In 1881 the Hewett family became involved in a scheme to form a new fish market at Shadwell, east London – in fact, it was the current owner of the business, Robert Hewett, who introduced a Private Act of Parliament to obtain the necessary legislation. For many years the facilities at Billingsgate, the central London fish market, had been notoriously inadequate and the time was ripe for competition. Needless to say, the Billingsgate authorities, the Fishmongers' Company (which made a good deal of money out of Billingsgate), and particularly the Corporation of London, which owned it, were formidable opponents of the scheme in Shadwell where there was more room and better communications by rail and road.

At a Parliamentary committee Hewett, supported by his son Robert jnr, gave some interesting statistics as to the extent of his business. He testified that in the previous seven years he had brought to London, mostly by boat, 1705 cargoes of fish amounting to 2,236,786 wooden boxes each containing 90lbs of fish – an annual average turnover of £280,000.

The scheme received Parliamentary approval in 1882, but financial investment did not materialise as hoped, and it was not until 1885 that the first piles were driven into the Thames for the market's construction. When it opened in November 1885 Hewett's Short Blue Fleet was the only supplier, and the company had guaranteed to bring all its catch to Shadwell for the next forty years – by 1898 Hewett had a fleet of 23 steamers and 147 smacks. It was not until 1893 that a second major fleet began delivering to Shadwell, and this was the highpoint of the project, for in 1895 the other supplier lost almost its entire fleet in a storm in the North Sea, and in 1899 disaster struck Hewett's. Though Hewett's had moved its fishing fleet up to Gorleston it still retained an engineering and repair business at Barking. In 1899 a boiler explosion destroyed the works there, killing ten men and injuring many more. One victim, blown clean through a wall, was not found until four days after the disaster. Over £2000 was raised to aid the bereaved families. Local schools gave children the day off "to show respect for the public funeral" of the victims.

The damage to Hewett's and also adjacent premises was expensive enough, but two years earlier a Workmen's Compensation Act had been passed to ensure adequate recompense in the

78. The explosion at Hewett's works on 6 January 1899.

79. The Town Quay in 1924.

event of death or injury to employees. An enquiry found that Hewett's had been negligent in their maintenance of the boiler, and they were made liable for damages under the Act. Unfortunately, they were not insured, and as a consequence the firm had to sell all its smacks. To make matters worse, only a few days after the explosion, the fleet lost one of its steamers – also uninsured.

By 1903 the last of the Barking fleet had been sold off. Meanwhile the Hewett business had switched from Gorleston to Yarmouth and in 1929 relocated to Fleetwood.

MARKET GARDENS AND MARSHLAND

Growing vegetables for the London market had begun by at least the mid-eighteenth century. A lease of 1732 mentions William Viveash of Barking, gardener, in relation to a 'Capital messuage called Coblers Hall, Garden and two cottages, at annual rent of £325 and a chine of pork and turkey at Christmas; alehouse called The Fighting Cocks with orchard and piece of ground at corner of Axe St., all in Barking at annual rent of 52s. 6d."

Writing in 1796 Lysons noted 300 acres planted with potatoes in the Barking area. By 1801 the potato acreage was just over a thousand, plus 330 acres planted with turnips or rape, 88 with peas and 51 with beans. The agricultural reformer and propagandist Arthur Young in 1807 declared that the largest potato-grower in Essex, possibly in England, was Mr T Pittman of Barking, who farmed from two to three hundred acres. His enterprise was skilfully integrated to take advantage of the opportunities open to him. Stable manure was brought from the capital by road and river to enrich his fields. Surplus potatoes were fed to a hundred oxen, accommodated in the largest "bullock house" in the county. He also spent two hundred pounds on digging a well to provide water to wash his potatoes before sending them to market. Pittman's fields followed a varying rotation of potatoes, clover and wheat.

Other major Barking crops were cabbages, turnips, asparagus, onions, cucumbers, strawberries, apples, plums, rhubarb and walnuts. Pruning, digging and trenching provided valuable off-season employment for locals. At harvest-time, when demand for labour was at a peak, girls were brought in from North Wales. Young also noted that inhabitants of Barking still enjoyed and exercised an ancient right to pasture cattle in Hainault Forest. Osiers were also still gathered in the marshlands for weaving into baskets.

Against this picture of diversified production and buoyant demand must be set evidence that even Barking's agricultural workers were not exempt from the general immiseration of rural labourers throughout southern England in the first four decades of the nineteenth century. In 1834 at Lodge Farm (*aka* Porters Lodge Farm), at the junction of Porters Avenue and Lodge Avenue, three stacks of wheat, rye and beans and a cart were fired during the night. The farm tenant was Henry Gray, the landowner Sir Charles Gray, Bart. An officer on horse patrol arrested two labourers, one carrying a steel and tinder.

Nor were the most progressive approaches universally followed. Amazingly in 1847 there was still a medieval open-field near Porters, on the Barking side of the Barking-Dagenham border. Its twenty-five acres were divided into eight strips, with three separate owners, although the whole area was actually farmed by Joseph and Philip Choat. These strips continued to appear on Ordnance Survey maps down to 1921.

By 1848 it was observed that "the market, held on Saturday, is now of trivial consequence but

80. *Gale Street Farm in 1905. Monochrome wash by A B Bamford.*

81. Moss Farm with the Power Station in the background, date unknown. The farm was on the south side of Ripple Road between Gale Street and the Ship and Shovel pub. It was notorious, even as late as the early 1960s, for the smell of pigs emanating from it.

here is an annual fair for cattle etc. on the 22nd of October ...". Some twenty farmers were listed then in Ripple Ward; most were tenants but two were noted as owners of their land. Eastbury House and Loxford Hall were also occupied by farmers. The continuing importance of agriculture to the local economy is further attested by the number of subsidiary occupations which depended on it – five corn dealers, six blacksmiths, three wheelwrights, three basket-makers, two leather cutters, a saddler, a millwright, a marshman, a tallow chandler, a cowkeeper and a cattle dealer.

Prominent among farming families were the Glennys. A Mrs Deborah Glenny is recorded as a market gardener as far back as 1796. In 1839 William and George Glenny had a market garden in Bull (now East) Street. A Francis Glenny was farming out at Chadwell Heath. In 1879 the 208 acre farm of William Wallis Glenny won second prize in a competition organized by the Royal Agricultural Society to encourage farmers in the

London area to grow more vegetables. In the 1880s Samuel Glenny was farming Greatfields in Ripple Road.

At Upney Farm, which extended over 102 acres in 1866, farmer Thomas Circuit introduced a style of cultivation, developed in Bedfordshire, of intercropping cucumbers and onions (some grown for seed) between rows of rye. Despite his progressive stance the farm was under pressure as a sales catalogue stressed that "the property being within eight miles of Town and only 20 minutes walk of Barking Station, it may let to much greater advantage as building sites." Nevertheless it was still being farmed in 1895.

MERINOS AND MILLING

About 1811 the park at Bifrons, some eighty acres in extent, was leased to Lord Somerville as grazing ground for his experimental herd of merino sheep.

John Southey Somerville (1765-1819) served as second president of the Board of Agriculture and,

82. *Uphall Farm, 1905. Watercolour by A B Bamford.*

with the personal encouragement of King George III, pioneered the introduction of the merino, publishing a treatise on the subject in 1803. The merino was to have a profound influence on the development of the woollen trade worldwide. Valued primarily for its thick lustrous fleece, rather than its meat, the merino had been for centuries a jealously guarded Spanish monopoly. Despite the best efforts of the Spanish to maintain their exclusive advantage the merino was smuggled out and, via France, George III was able to obtain enough sheep to establish a royal herd at Windsor in 1788. Twenty years later, in gratitude for British assistance against the invading French, the Spanish sent four thousand merinos to the king as a gift. It may well be that the Bifrons herd came from that importation. It was certainly in 1811 that a Merino Society was founded to encourage cross-breeding with native strains to develop more productive hybrid types.

As in many areas on the fringe of London with water access and an arable hinterland, milling remained a significant local business. In 1738 Jeremiah Bentham, father of the philosopher Jeremy Bentham, bought a brick malthouse which stood beside a windmill behind the site of the Fishing Smack public house. The eminent engineer John Smeaton (1724-94) is known to have designed the gearing system for a windmill at Barking. Wellington Mill, built and patriotically so called in 1815, stood eighty yards south of London Road and just east of Back River. It was first occupied by fisherman John Brown. In 1824 miller Richard Turpin was killed when a sudden squall turned the sail that he was working on, carrying him up only to fall to an instant death at the feet of his wife, who had rushed to help him on hearing him cry out. The mill was converted to electricity in 1906 and demolished in 1926.

Although the expansion of housing would inexorably diminish the cultivated area around Barking with increasing rapidity from the 1880s, it was not until the construction of the Becontree estate in the inter-war period that the last substantial farms in the immediate area would disappear under the flood-tide of bricks and mortar.

83. *Wellington Mill, a smock mill, probably about 1895. It was built south of London Road and east of the Back River, in 1815 (hence its name).*

The Advent of Industry

The excavations just outside the abbey precincts in 1996, revealing tenth century Saxon workshops, enable Barking, in at least a broad sense, to lay claim to an industrial heritage stretching back over a millennium. The building and repairing of ships was certainly established locally by Tudor times and, if farming and fishing remained the basis of the local economy, processing their products gave rise to such employments as brewing, baking, tanning and milling.

FORCES FOR CHANGE
Industry in Barking in its modern sense, however, dates back some two centuries, its advent heralded by improvements in local communications. In1809 a turnpike trust was established for the road from the East India Docks to Barking. This Commercial Road Trust in 1810 built the first iron bridge in Essex to carry the new route over the river Lea. Around 1810 the Tilbury Fort Turnpike Trust, aiming to improve communica-

tions between Tilbury and the newly-built docks in east London, upgraded the whole Tilbury Road, including what is now Ripple Road. In 1854 the London, Tilbury & Southend Railway opened as far as Tilbury, reaching Southend in 1856. In 1858 a link was opened between Barking and Bow, and in 1885-8 a new line was built from Barking to Pitsea.

Another factor encouraging the emergence of local industry was the passage of legislation to control pollution in London, which forced many manufacturers to seek relocation elsewhere. As the former market gardens of the East End disappeared, the presence of industrial facilities, particularly those engaged in noxious trades, became increasingly intolerable and were vilified by the new breed of local bureaucrat, the Medical Officer of Health and the Borough Surveyor or Engineer, as a public nuisance and hazard to health.

EARLY INDUSTRIES
In 1809 local Barking inventor James Grellier patented "A building of a Peculiar Construction for the purpose of burning coke and lime, whereby the Superfluous Heat of the Fire used in Burning the Coke is applied to Burn the Lime, and also

84. A watermill owned by the Abbey is mentioned in the Domesday Survey of 1086. The flour mills were bought by Ridley & Sons in 1862, and closed at the end of the 19th century.

whereby such Fire may be rendered Perpetual, which I therein denominated The Union and Perpetual Kiln." In the same year, in partnership with John Passman he established a Roman Cement and Plaster of Paris factory on the Isle of Dogs. Although it soon passed out of their hands it did become the largest plaster works in Britain before being taken over in 1867 by J.B. Lawes *(see below)*, who converted it to the production of citric and tartaric acid.

In 1836-7 a gas works for Barking was established at a cost of £1,500 raised in shares of five pounds each. Intended purely to supply the locality it was but a feeble foretaste of much greater things to come.

A Barking Iron Foundry is known to have been in existence by 1866, when only three of 23 known Essex foundries were in Barking and West Ham. By 1890 nine of 29 would be. In 1902 the Wedlake foundry of Hornchurch moved to Barking as the London Scottish Foundry.

A brewery run by a member of the Glenny family was in existence by 1871. It had fifteeen tied houses and was taken over by Taylor Walker in 1930.

Most of the industries attracted to Barking, however, were based on chemical products or processes. Between 1862 and 1882 Edward Steane ran a soap factory in Fisher Street. Edward Crow made chemicals at Barking Creek from 1862 but by 1895 had transferred its operations both there and at Bromley-by-Bow to Harts Marshes at the end of Harts Lane. The Davey family operated a tar distillery on Barking Creek between 1878 and 1906. By 1878 Daniel de Pass had opened his Barking Guano Works at Creekmouth. In 1885 Barking Magazine was sold off by the government to the Creekmouth Gunpowder Company, although it remained under military guard.

A BIG STINK

The prevalence of market gardening in the Barking area created a demand for London's waste in all its forms to renew the fertility of intensively cultivated soil. By the mid-nineteenth century these inputs, ranging from night-soil to slaughter-house refuse and dead animals, were being unloaded from barges at the Town Quay and carted through the streets to noisome effect. In 1851 a public petition against this practice led to an official inquiry by the government's recently established General Board of Health. This provoked a counter-petition claiming that the practice had been general for a century, that the previous year's throughput of two hundred cargoes of manure had been worth a thousand pounds to the local economy and that, if they

85. A sewage farm at Lodge Farm, run by the Metropolis and Essex Reclamation Company, set up to process London sewage for use in agriculture and horticulture. From The Illustrated London News *26 September 1868.*

could not be manured, the market gardens would have to be put to less labour-intensive grain crops, which would cost up to eighty labourers their jobs. The final outcome was continued toleration of the practice but within tighter regulations to control the hours and manner of traffic.

A decade later the construction of the capital's first modern sewerage system in 1861-2 by Sir Joseph Bazalgette, Chief Engineer of the Metropolitan Board of Works, opened up an entirely new possibility of fertiliser supply, totally superseding the barges and carts of the past. His massive Northern Outfall sewer deposited all the waste from northern London on the west side of Barking Creek, hopefully to be carried away by the tide of the Thames. As a contemporary noted "It was certainly an improvement for the residents of London but it made life very unpleasant on occasions in Barking."

John Morton of Lodge Farm, Barking soon began processing 300,000 tons of London sewage into manure. This operation was taken over in 1866 by the Metropolis Sewage and Essex Reclamation Co. and in 1867 John Morton was replaced as manager by Henry L Petre. By 1868, 360,000 tons of London sewage were being applied to 120 acres of land, about half the farm, as fertilizer for rye grass, sugar beet, cereals and the common horticultural crops of the vicinity – potatoes, cabbages, beans, onions, carrots and strawberries.

Bazalgette's optimistic assumption that the tidal action of the Thames would dispose of the discharge of the Northern Outfall proved ill-founded. To the contrary, much 'excrementious matter' was swept onshore. The banks of Barking Creek became lined with dense layers of slime, fat and offal up to nine feet deep. The river itself became permanently polluted with a suspension of filth which, in 1878 contributed to worsening still further the immense loss of life resulting from the sinking of the pleasure steamer *Princess Alice*. Returning from Sheerness, packed with some seven hundred passengers, the vessel was just entering Gallions Reach when it collided with a massive steel collier, five times its size, which sliced the *Princess Alice* clean in two. As passengers swam for their lives even the strongest found themselves choked or sucked under by the lethal sludge. Onshore at Creekmouth local people at a summer fête could clearly hear the cries of the doomed but were powerless to do more than help ashore the few who made it that far. Only 69 of the day-trippers survived. The exact death-toll remains unknown but was probably between 590 and 640, making it the worst inshore shipping disaster in Britain's entire history. Bodies subse-

86. *Recovery of bodies after the* sinking of the Princess Alice *off Gallions Reach. About 600 people perished. From* The Illustrated London News *14 Sept. 1878.*

quently recovered from the river were taken to temporary morgues at Creekmouth, the watermen who brought them in being rewarded at the rate of five shillings per corpse. A national collection raised 23,000 donations of sixpence to put up a memorial cross in Woolwich cemetery. Gallions Reach subsequently became known as Haunted Reach. A Board of Trade enquiry found the experienced Captain Grinstead of the *Princess Alice* responsible for the catastrophe. He was among the drowned.

In 1884 a Royal Commission discovered that there was still so much fat being deposited in the Creekmouth area that seven men gained their livelihood by skimming it off to be melted down for resale. Improved sewage treatment facilities were at last installed in 1887-9 but a decade later local dignitary W W Glenny could still complain that "The Roding ... has degenerated into an open sewer; from a living current it has been converted into a fetid ditch, a receiver for the filth and abomination of the district and a source of danger and dismay to the inhabitants." To be fair, however, it must be conceded that the bulk of such

pollution was by then locally generated rather than transferred from the capital.

THINKING BIG: FERTILISER

In 1857 a factory was built by the Lawes Chemical Manure Company at Creekmouth to manufacture artificial fertilizer and sulphuric acid. The venture was founded by Sir John Bennett Lawes (1814-1900) of Rothamsted, Herts. Educated at Eton, he left Oxford without a degree, the university at that time being incapable of serving his scientific interests. On coming of age and inheriting the family estate Lawes set up a laboratory at home and experimented enthusiastically but aimlessly until a neighbour's chance remark drew his attention to the value of animal bones as a fertiliser for turnips. Lawes obtained splendid results by dressing his crops with bones dissolved in sulphuric acid, which released their phosphate content. Taking out a patent on his discovery in 1842, he set up his first factory at Deptford the following year. In that same year, 1843, he established an agricultural experiment station at Rothamsted, financing its work from the profits of the business.

The Creekmouth venture was very much larger in scale and benefited from its proximity to the recently completed railway line to London. By the 1890s it would employ over four hundred men. Lawes himself sold out his interest in the fertiliser business in 1872, although he remained involved in the chemical business, as well as continuing his Rothamsted experiments. Concentrating on problems of crop rotation and animal nutrition Lawes and his chief collaborator, J H Gilbert, published 132 separate papers or reports in the course of their joint career. Lawes' contributions to agriculture were recognised by honorary degrees from Edinburgh, Oxford and Cambridge, the Fellowship of the Royal Society and a baronetcy.

One of Lawes' employees at Barking was Robert Warington (1838-1907) who had literally grown up in Apothecaries' Hall. His father sent him to work for a year as Lawes' unpaid assistant at Rothamsted. In 1867 Warington was appointed chemist to Lawes' works at Barking, a post he retained until 1874. He later became Sibthorpian professor of agriculture at Oxford. Warington's *Chemistry of the Farm* reached its 19th English edition in his own lifetime and was translated into several foreign languages.

87. *Advertisement for Lawes' Chemical Manure Co.*

LAWES
Chemical Manure Co., Ltd.
(ESTABLISHED 1842).

AERIAL PHOTO OF WORKS.

Manufacturers of FERTILISERS
SHEEP DIPS, DISINFECTANTS
FUMIGANTS, INSECTICIDES, etc.

Head Office and Works   -   CREEKSMOUTH, BARKING, ESSEX
Telegrams: "Rothamsted, Barking."   *Telephone:* Grangewood 0290.

BRANCHES   -   -   -   GLASGOW, PERTH, AND CHANNEL ISLES

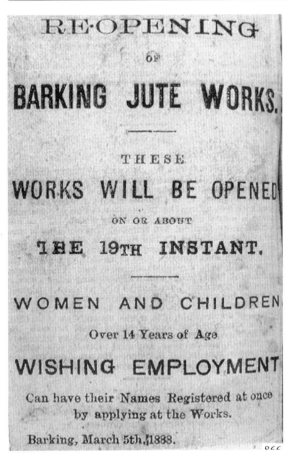

88. The re-opening jute works in 1888, from the Essex Times in March that year.

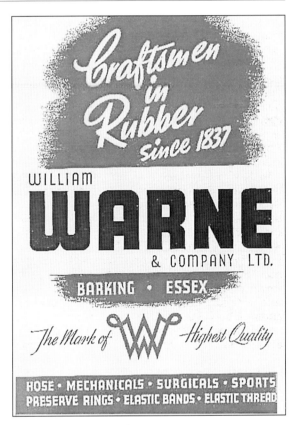

89. Advertisement for Warne's, manufacturers of rubber goods, who took over the jute factory in 1895.

THINKING BIG: JUTE

In 1866 the world's largest jute factory was opened in Fisher Street (now Abbey Road). The man behind the venture was Thomas Duff, who was connected with the jute industry in Dundee, where it had been first established in Britain in the 1830s. The imposing building he erected, the first large-scale fireproof mill in Essex, housed 1,600 workers – overwhelmingly women and boys. Employment prospects for locals were limited by their lack of appropriate skills and in consequence it proved necessary to import girls from Dundee, the home of the jute industry. Making the jute up into bags and sacks gave further employment in the town. In the factory the normal shift lasted twelve hours, from six in the morning till six at night, with a break for breakfast and twenty minutes for lunch. Competition from India soon put the business under pressure. Ownership changed hands. There were strikes. Irish girls

were imported as cheap labour. The depression of the mid-1880s hit particularly hard and the factory closed down completely in May 1886. The Revd Thomas Davies, minister of Barking's Congregational church, established a Jute Girls' Distress Fund, which collected cash and gifts in kind to provide a thousand free meals, pay rents and, most radically, pay for the passage and outfit for 35 girls to emigrate to Canada. Even though the jute factory finally reopened in March 1888 the industry eventually proved unviable. Following strikes and a lock-out, the works closed for good in 1891. Once again the Congregationalists organised relief which enabled 'foreign' employees, most recently brought in as strike-breakers, to get home to Scotland and Ireland, though others went on to a new life in Canada. A number of more senior employees established themselves in business locally. Engineer Thomas Young worked his way up from repairing houses and collecting rents to become an auctioneer and estate agent. Mr Donaldson, the last manager, opened an

90. *An aerial view of Beckton gas works c.1952.*

engineering works. J W Garland became a prosperous greengrocer. One of the foremen opened a bag and sack factory.

William Warne and Co. (founded in 1837 as The London Caotchouc Co.), manufacturers of rubber goods bought the jute factory premises in 1895. Here they developed a diverse output of specialised products, ranging from food-sealing rings and football bladders to roller-covers for the printing industry, from catheters, tubes and sheeting for use in hospitals to elasticated thread for corsets and suspenders.

THINKING BIG: GAS

In 1867 a new statutory gas supply company, the Gas Light and Coke Company, was formed with the object of building the world's largest gas works on five hundred acres of open marshland between East Ham and Barking. Its riverside location would greatly facilitate the unloading of the vast amounts of coal consumed by the gas works furnaces but also meant that for decades its labour force would be faced night and morning with a dreary trudge over unmade, unlit pathways through a dismal landscape.

Construction of what was to become the Beckton Gas Works was entrusted to William Aird (1833-1911), whose father, a Scottish mason, had settled at Bromley-by-Bow and built up a contracting business, laying down gas and water mains. At the age of eighteen Aird had been entrusted with

disassembling the Crystal Palace and re-erecting it at Sydenham. Aird's later projects – reservoirs, gasworks, waterworks, railways and docks – would span the globe, from Berlin to Brazil, from Copenhagen to Calcutta. His greatest enterprise would be the damming of the Nile at Aswan, but Beckton was certainly challenge enough for a man in his thirties. Named for Simon Adam Beck of the Gas Light and Coke Company, the plant came into commission in 1870. Serviced by its own internal railway system, Beckton provided work for over a thousand Barking men.

STRIKE!

The remarkable success of the gas workers' strike at Beckton in 1889 did not emerge from a vacuum but occurred against a background of recurrent, intermittent, bouts of labour militancy.

In 1872 two workers at the Beckton works, Edward Jones and Thomas Dilley, petitioned the management for a sixpence per day rise for the coal wheelers employed there. The next day Dilley was given seven days' notice. The workers, led by Jones, went on strike, demanding Dilley's reinstatement. Jones and four others were then prosecuted and sentenced at the Old Bailey to twelve months for "conspiring, with threats, to coerce the Beckton Gas Company." The families of the imprisoned men were supported by funds from a Gas Stokers' Defence Committee, which also sent a letter of appeal to the Home Secretary.

91. Will Thorne.

As a result the sentences were reduced to four months.

Attempts were made to form a union at Beckton in 1884 and again in 1885. Both failed. The deep depression of 1886, which caused Barking's jute factory to close, scuppered the prospects of any further attempt at militant action.

In March 1889 large-scale lay-offs were made at Beckton Gas Works. A protest meeting was organised for Sunday 31 March. Scheduled for the working man's only day of rest, it was able to attract support from gas workers from other parts of the capital. The speakers included Will Thorne (1857-1946), the son of a Birmingham bricklayer, whose working life had started at the age of six. Still illiterate at his marriage in 1879, Thorne had started working at Beckton in 1884 and joined the Canning Town branch of the Social Democratic Federation. A fellow member of the SDF, Karl Marx's daughter Eleanor, taught Thorne to read and write, so well indeed that he became branch secretary. He repaid Eleanor's efforts by naming one of his sons Karl. Through the SDF Thorne met such leading left-wing luminaries as H M Hyndman, George Bernard Shaw and Friedrich Engels. He also developed into a powerful public speaker. In an age of outdoor mass-meetings this has to be taken literally. Lung-power was quite as important as eloquence when addressing mass-meetings in the open air and Thorne was a big, powerfully built man.

At the March 31st meeting Thorne pledged that if the gas workers formed themselves into a union and stood solid against the employers within six months they could win an eight-hour day and a six-day week. At the meeting a committee, including Thorne, Ben Tillett and William Byford, was formed to organise the union and eight hundred men were recruited on the spot, paying a membership fee of a shilling each. By dispensing with the Benefit Fund of a craft union they were able to set the weekly subscription at a minimal threshold of twopence a week. Ben Tillett (1860-1943) a Bristolian, had been a child acrobat in a circus, a shoemaker, a sailor and a docker. A Christian Socialist and ardent Temperance campaigner, Tillett found an appropriate niche as general secretary of the Tea Operatives and General Labourers' Association. In 1888 he had led an unsuccessful strike at Tilbury docks. Tillett stood against Thorne for the post of general secretary of the new union but it was Thorne who was elected. Byford became treasurer. (Following the death of his first wife, Thorne would marry Byford's daughter, Emily.)

When the committee was enlarged some members were for demanding a pay rise of a shilling a day but Thorne argued for the reduction of the working day from twelve hours to eight, not only for the immediate benefit of the existing labour force but because "it meant a large number of unemployed would be absorbed and so reduce the inhuman competition that was making men more like beasts than civilized persons." New recruits would, it was hoped, also become loyal members of the union which had, in effect, created their jobs.

Thorne proved to be a masterly negotiator and the eight-hour day was won within a matter of weeks, not months, and without even having to call a strike. Membership of the Gasworkers' Union expanded to 20,000 and their success inspired the historic London dockers' strike led by Tillett later that same year, Thorne being the main speaker at the meeting which launched the strike. Many dockworkers, moreover, had themselves often been employed in the gasworks during the winter months when the demand for casual labour on the wharves fell off. The dockers' success, building on that of the Gasworkers, inaugurated a new era in labour history as the 'New Unionism' mobilised the ranks of the previously unorganised unskilled masses. In the

92. *An undated photograph of a scene at R. White's mineral water factory in Axe Street. White's took over the celebrated Van mineral water company.*

January 1890 issue of the monthly magazine *Time* Thorne and Mark Hutchins, the Union's President, sketched out their objectives, strategy and success to date:

" ... our Union is going to show that the unskilled workers must henceforth be reckoned with; it will show both employers and the aristocrats of labour that they are the real power. For this reason the Gas workers' is also a General Labourers' Union. Moreover it is wholly and solely a fighting body. Our Union is not to degenerate into a mere burial and benefit society.... Our Union is also one of the very few in which men and women are on equal terms... Female Branches – and very flourishing ones – have been organised in London and Bristol... The work we have done in less than twelve months is this. We have enrolled over 50,000 workers, hitherto absolutely unorganised. We have gained for 80,000 men an eight instead of a twelve hour working day, which means - to take only the East End of London – the employment of 5,000 more men this winter, i.e. some 20,000 less starving men, women and children."

Thorne went on to serve West Ham as councillor or alderman for over fifty years and as MP for West Ham from 1906 and for Plaistow from 1918 until his death. Tillett became general secretary of the General Labourers' Union, a leading Fabian and a founder of the Independent Labour Party, the Labour Party and the *Daily Herald*.

ANOTHER GASSY PRODUCT

In 1876 H F Van opened a coffee-shop in Heath Street and began making his own mineral waters. As this side-line soon overshadowed the original business Van built a factory in Axe Street where Bifrons House had once stood. Claimed to be the largest mineral water factory in London, it was designed to enable delivery vans to drive straight through, unloading empties and loading up with fresh stock. In 1886 Van opened a branch at Grays but this overstretched his resources and in 1890 he sold out to R White & Sons, who improved the Axe Street premises and became a public company in 1894. The factory was finally demolished in 1972-3 when White's relocated to East Ham.

Churches and Churchmen

THE PARISH CHURCH

St Margaret's appears to have originated as a chapel in the twelfth century and to have been elevated to the status of parish church around 1300 at the initiative of the then abbess, Anne de Vere. The chancel and part of the nave date from at least the early thirteeenth century. Probably from this period also is the remnant of black marble slab from the north chapel which carries fragmentary inscriptions apparently commemorating Maurice, who was bishop of London in 1086-1107 and Aelfgiva, who was abbess of Barking in 1066. The slab may have come from the abbey but was in the church since at least the eighteenth century.

Major alterations in the fifteenth century added the tower, vestry and north and south chapels. In the early sixteenth century the outer north aisle and a north porch were added. Dating various parts of the structure is complicated by the fact that alterations were often made by the recycling of older materials.

Normally in the fourteenth century there were two vicars, one to serve the town, the other the abbey church. An incised monument to Martin the Vicar, showing his vestments and dated 1328, was uncovered in the abbey excavations of 1911-12. A brass of a priest in academic robes has been dated to *c.*1480.

Despite the relative autonomy parish status conferred, the church stood within the abbey precincts and remained liable to its interference. Between 1358 and 1376, for example, it was ordered that the vicar and his parishioners should join in the major service held in the abbey church annually on 13 July to commemorate the day of its dedication. As the disastrous floods of the latter decade plunged the abbey into financial crisis it was decided, probably over the objections of the townspeople, to merge the two posts of vicar into one. This was the situation from 1398 onwards. It did not always work smoothly. In 1414 the abbess had to appeal to Rome to oblige the vicar to say Mass in the abbey church as he was bound to do. In 1452 the vicar's terms of remuneration were revised. Instead of receiving a hog, a lamb, a goose and a cheese he was to

93. *A priest at Barking, 1485.*

receive three yards of cloth and daily meals at the convent for himself and his servant, which sounds generous enough but may have been another way of exerting some control over his daily routine.

After the dissolution the rectory and the right to appoint to the vicarage (advowson) passed to the Crown and then through various hands until purchased in 1557 by the executors of William Pownsett and presented to All Souls College, Oxford. In 1583 the Crown contested this, possibly on the grounds that the 1557 arrangements included a requirement for weekly prayers for Pownsett and his nominees and were therefore to be condemned as 'superstitious uses'. The Crown therefore nominated Edward Edgeworth, chaplain to the Queen's favourite, Robert Dudley, Earl of Leicester. A lawsuit eventually resulted in his ejection in 1587 and the reassertion of All Souls' rights. Edgeworth went on to Ireland to become bishop of Down and Connor.

For Thomas Cartwright (1634-89) the vicarage at Barking was to prove a stepping-stone to much greater things – but one he was careful to retain – and also, ultimately to Ireland. The son of a

94. *St Margaret's Church from the north-east, c.1800.*

95. *One of the earliest photographs of Barking shows St Margaret's Church and churchyard in 1860.*

96. A window in St Margaret's depicts the Barking fishing industry. (Photo: Donald S Parsons)

97. View of the nave and screen in St Margaret's. In 1770-71 the open timber roof was covered with an ornamental plaster ceiling. This was removed during subsequent renovations.

Brentwood schoolmaster and grandson of a prominent puritan of Elizabeth's reign, Cartwright studied at Oxford when it was under puritan domination and served as chaplain at Queen's College before becoming vicar of Walthamstow, where he established a reputation as a "very forward and confident preacher for the cause then in being". This did not inhibit him from becoming an ardent royalist at the Restoration and within months obtaining the appointment of vicar of Barking. Other preferments followed – prebendary of St Paul's, of Wells and of Durham and dean of Ripon. Cartwright became a great favourite of James, Duke of York. When the duke became king as James II he nominated Cartwright to the vacant see of Chester, while allowing him to keep his Barking living and another one at Wigan. Cartwright was deeply implicated in plotting to restore Catholicism and supported James's absolutist pretensions, notably by trying to force his nominee for the presidency of Magdalen College, Oxford on the resistant Fellows. He also tried to use his royal connections to pressure All Souls into allowing him to hand over the Barking vicarage to one of his numerous sons. Cartwright's totally mistaken judgment of clergy attitudes to the king's policies and consequently misleading advice to the monarch proved crucial to James's overthrow. Cartwright himself fled to James's exiled court in France, then followed him to Ireland, where he died of dysentery, refusing a deathbed conversion to Catholicism.

The fabric of St Margaret's continued to undergo alterations. A richly carved stone font was added in about 1635 and a three-decker pulpit in 1727. In 1698 the vestry was embellished with new panelling through the generosity of the Bertie family, who had also donated an alms-dish, a cup, two patens and two flagons. In 1769 a new organ was installed (rebuilt 1855 and 1913). In 1770-71 the whole interior was plastered, elaborate coved ceilings inserted in nave and chancel and the windows remodelled at the behest of Bamber Gascoyne of Bifrons, who allegedly declare that God's house should be at least as handsome as his own. Most of these alterations were removed in subsequent restorations. That

98. The Glenny family headstone in St Margaret's churchyard.

of 1842 involved the demolition of the Cambell family chapel of 1645, the relocation of the pulpit and removal of its sounding-board, and the renovation of the pews to incorporate eighteenth-century woodwork. A wooden font cover was provided at this time, the work of the royal wood-carver W G Rogers (1792-1875). Further alterations were made in 1889 and 1907-13 and another major restoration undertaken in 1928, when a stained-glass window was inserted to commemorate the vanished glories of the local fishing industry.

Impressive funereal monuments in varying styles were added by local gentry. The wealthy grazier William Pownsett (1554) had an altar tomb in the north aisle. John and Elizabeth Tedcastell (1596) and their numerous progeny – nine sons and seven daughters – were commemorated by a brass. Wall tablets were preferred for Elizabeth Hobart (1590) and Francis Fuller (1636). The marble monument of sea-captain John Bennett (1706) features a portrait bust and ships. The monument to John Bamber of Bifrons (1753) has been attributed to the great Roubiliac. Others commemorate Sir Orlando Humphreys (1737), Sir Crisp Gascoyne (1761) and members of the Fanshawe and Bertie families. The inimitable architectural critic Ian Nairn awarded the palm to the memorial of Sir Charles Montagu (1625) which moved him to a characteristic flight of fancy and an emphatic verdict:

"a faery scene: a camp before battle, Sir Charles seated and pensive, a ferocious rifleman on either side, tents fading away into the back of the picture.

Yet he died at his home, aged sixty-one. Is it all allegorical, man waiting reflectively in purgatory for the battle at the Last Judgement? This is what it feels like, extremely atmospheric and poetic and a huge reproach to all the hack-work which passes for early seventeenth century sculpture in Britain."

Although Ilford was established as a separate parish in 1830, there was no further sub-division of Barking before World War One. To cope with the local growth of population, however, a mission hall was built in Fisher Street in 1878, a mission church opened at Creekmouth by 1894 and a chapel at ease, dedicated to St. Paul, built (1893-1914) to the designs of Sir Arthur Blomfield in Ripple Road on a site donated by the Marquess of Salisbury.

St Margaret's vicarage house stood in East Street until it was replaced by a new one, north of Ripple Road in 1794. The East Street building was finally demolished in 1935.

DISSENT

The, admittedly imperfect, religious census of the province of Canterbury conducted in 1676 revealed that in the Deanery of Barking, consisting of thirty parishes (less the seven which failed to make returns) there were 3,369 Conformists, 94 Nonconformists and 12 Papists.

A Presbyterian conventicle is said to have met at the Barking house of one William Taylor in 1676. He may be identical with Richard Taylor (died 1697) a minister to a Congregational meeting and a man wealthy enough to keep a coach. Barking figures in a list of dissenting meetings of 1715-16 but there appear to be no later references to such a congregation.

QUAKERS

In 1672 the Society of Friends bought half an acre of orchard from Edward Burling for use as a burial ground. The following year they paid £87 for an adjacent mansion known as Tates Place, whose Great Hall they could use for worship. It was partly rebuilt by them in 1758.

The Quakers appear to have represented a periodically troublesome presence. In 1705 when a Barking Quakeress was being interred in Barking churchyard at the request of her son, the Norwegian-born itinerant preacher and pamphleteer Christopher Meidel joined local Quakers in their graveside protest against the

99. The Friends Meeting House in North Street, by A B Bamford, 1905.

burial ceremony. Meidel harangued the crowd until forcefully ejected by the vicar's son. Soon afterwards Meidel was in Chelmsford gaol.

Richard Claridge (1649-1723), a local schoolmaster from 1702 to 1707, refused to pay church rates or serve as a parish officer and had his goods distrained as a result.

A number of leading Barking Quakers were, however, men of substance. John Fowke (d. 1691) of Claybury was a major landowner and the son of a former Lord Mayor. William Mead (1628-1713), who made a fortune as a London linendraper, became a personal friend of George Fox, was famously imprisoned with William Penn and met the king to represent the Quaker cause. He purchased the manor of Gooshays in Havering and bequeathed a £100 to the Barking meeting.

In 1766 Quakers were still the largest of the local dissenting groups but they diminished thereafter, largely through their refusal to countenance any of their number marrying out of their Society. The Barking meeting closed down as a regular congregation in 1830. Although the meeting-house was used occasionally thereafter it was recorded as disused by 1848. The burial ground in North Street was also retained and in 1845 witnessed a major public occasion in the interment of the celebrated Quaker prison reformer Elizabeth Fry (1780-1845). Her brother, the financier and philanthropist Samuel Gurney (1786-1856) was subsequently buried nearby. The Barking Meeting was revived in 1891 and in 1908 a new Friends' Meeting House was built in Queen Anne style.

BAPTISTS

Barking Baptists are known to have met in houses licensed for the purpose between 1692 and 1711 but no later references have been found for this congregation. A Baptist presence was re-established in Ilford from the 1790s onwards and it was with their help that a Barking church was formally established in 1850 and a building erected in Queen's Road in 1851-2. In 1893 the congregation built the Tabernacle in Linton Road, selling off their original home to the Peculiar People. Upney Baptist Church began as an off-shoot of the Tabernacle. Baptists were also to be found during the 1940s running a Sunday school at the then isolated Maybell farm house on Castle Green in Ripple Road.

CONGREGATIONALISTS

The early Congregationalist presence appears to have fizzled out and therefore lacks any direct connection with the re-establishment of Congregationalism by George Gold of West Ham in a hired house in 1782. Formally constituted as a church in 1785, its members then erected a

101. *Maybell House on Castle Green, Ripple Road, used by Baptists for a Sunday school in the 1940s.*

100. *The Baptist Tabernacle in Linton Road, c.1916.*

102. *A Baptist Tabernacle outing in 1923, in a horse brake. The Reverend and Mrs Taylor can be seen on the front seat.*

meeting-house in the Broadway. This was enlarged in 1805. As minister from 1804 to 1818 J. Kennet Parker attracted some fifty new members. By 1829 the congregation was estimated at 350-400. A new and larger building was erected in 1864 and new schoolrooms added in 1877. The Broadway site was sold off after World War One and in 1929 a new building was put up in Upney Lane.

METHODISTS

John Cennick (1718-55), an early disciple of Wesley but subsequently a pastor in the Moravian church, appears to have caused a major stir in Barking with his preaching around 1750 but this failed to result in the formation of any new church. Methodism as such came to Barking in 1781 with open air preaching by Wesley's lieutenant, Thomas Coke (1747-1814). Wesley himself visited Barking in 1783 and again in 1784. In 1785 Barking's Anglican curate, Isaac Peach, was suspended for allegedly lacking the 'weight and influence' needed to combat the rising tide of Methodism. Local opinion was said to be much impressed by the fate of a local inn-keeper who had used a

mounting-block as an improvised pulpit to parody Methodist preaching, promising to repeat his performance the following Sunday – by which time he was dead and buried.

Soho shoemaker John Childs sent six of his workmen to live and preach at Barking to consolidate the Methodist presence. By 1791 it was part of the First London circuit, headquartered at City Road, Wesley's own chapel. In 1824 it became part of the new Spitalfields circuit and in 1833 was attached to Romford. A wooden chapel was occupied in Bull Street, the western end of East Street. Although the congregation dwindled from twenty to eleven to three by 1825 the Sunday school had 59 children in attendance. A Reform group broke away in 1851 and in 1869 the original core built a new chapel. In 1928 a Central Hall was built on the opposite (north) side of East Street thanks to a £30,000 donation from milling magnate and future movie mogul J Arthur Rank. Ironically, or perhaps not, the old chapel was demolished and the Capitol cinema built on its site.

A Primitive Methodist church existed in Manor Road by 1861 and was closed by 1933.

ROMAN CATHOLICS
In 1858 a church dedicated to St Ethelburga was opened in temporary premises at the back of the Red Lion pub in Station (later Linton) Road. By 1863 services were being held in the Roman Catholic school. In 1869 the church of SS Mary and Ethelburga in Linton Road was dedicated.

THE SALVATION ARMY
In 1873 a building at Town Quay called the Old Bethel was opened as station number 15 of William Booth's Christian Mission. In 1875 Miss Anne Davies was appointed as its commandant. Captain Skidmore became the first officer of a Barking Corps in 1878. By 1889 the Army had moved on to a hall in Ripple Road. Rebuilt in 1922, burned down in 1934 and rebuilt in 1935, it was destroyed by bombing in 1941 and rebuilt again in 1951.

MISSION AT SEA
The Mission to Deep Sea Fishermen was founded at Barking in 1881 by Ebenezer J. Mather, who had been shocked by the conditions he found among men working the Dogger Bank – high accident rates, coupled with inadequate medical provision and worsened by the activities of 'copers', ships selling cheap grog to the fishermen. In 1882 Mather fitted out the fishing smack *Ensign* to carry medical supplies, Bibles, warm woollen clothing and tobacco for the comfort of the men of the deep sea fleets. By 1887 an international convention had driven the copers from the seas. In 1896 the Mission's efforts were recognised and rewarded with Royal Patronage.

RISING STARS
Herbert Hensley Henson (1863-1947) was vicar of Barking for only seven years, which proved to be an arduous and sometimes controversial passage in a long and distinguished career. After what he considered "an unhappy and ill-ordered boyhood" and an interrupted education, he managed to enter Oxford as a non-collegiate student. A first in history led on to a Fellowship at All Souls. Ordained deacon, Henson at 24 became head of Oxford House, a university mission at Bethnal Green. A year later, ordained priest, he was appointed by his college to the living at Barking. At his first meeting with the churchwardens he noticed a strong smell of gas in the church. Upon enquiry it was explained to him that the problem had been attended to several times by a gasfitter member of the congre-

gation but without success. Henson asked if there was anyone else and was told that there was but that he was an atheist. Henson demanded that he be sent for on the grounds that technical competence was the more relevant qualification in the circumstances.

Henson believed that the laity were increasingly wary of the church and of clergymen and indifferent to theological subtleties – but they did respect Jesus. His own desire to proclaim the gospel with clarity led him to promote the use of the Revised version of the Bible, despite the disapproval of his diocesan and suffragan bishops. Within a year of his arrival he had pitched himself into a furious local controversy over the election of a local school board. In 1890 he threw open the grounds of the vicarage for a Barking Elementary Schools Treat, which began with a brass band procession through the town and ended with tea in three sittings for a staggering 2,350 children. This initiative immediately became an institution. By 1895 the number of children reached 3,600. Henson also instituted an annual parade for the gasworkers and gave lunch hour talks in the Beckton canteen. Within six years he had built up a congregation four hundred strong at St Margaret's.

The Barking years proved arduous, strained Henson's health and left little time for reading but his efforts brought him to the notice of the Prime Minister, Lord Salisbury who appointed him to the chaplaincy of Ilford Hospital in 1895.

By 1900 he would be a canon of Westminster Abbey and ultimately bishop, first of Hereford, then of Durham. A brilliant preacher, fearless controversialist and an accomplished writer, he surveyed his career in an autobiography whose self-effacing title – *Retrospect of an Unimportant Life* – was rather belied by the fact that it ran to three volumes.

Glaswegian Leslie Stannard Hunter (1890-1983), vicar of Barking from 1926 to 1930, came with experience of the YMCA, as a hospital chaplain, from working with art students and a five-year spell on Tyneside. These varied challenges, confirmed by his years in Barking, issued in *A Parson's Job* (1931) in which he argued the case for a strongly led team ministry as the most effective approach to the problems and needs of increasingly secularized communities. He subsequently became bishop of Sheffield.

James Theodore Inskip (1868-1949) served the people of Barking for almost thirty years as suffragan bishop. A Bristolian by birth, he served

103. James Carmel Heenan (centre) was the curate at the Roman Catholic church in Linton Road after his ordination in 1930. He became Archbishop of Westminster in 1963, and was created Cardinal in 1965.

in Leyton, Newcastle and Southport before his translation to Barking in 1919. An eminent educationist as well as churchman, he took a keen interest in local schools and represented his old university, Cambridge, on many educational bodies. He wrote on pastoral work and evangelicalism and composed an autobiography, *A Man's Job* (1948).

His Eminence John Carmel Heenan (1905-75) was born in Ilford of Irish parents. Ordained in 1930, from 1931 to 1937 he worked as curate at the church of SS Mary & Ethelburga in Linton Road. It is said that on his very first day in Barking he was appalled to see a gaggle of nuns smoking – until he discovered that they were extras in the Barking historical pageant. In 1936 Heenan visited the Soviet Union, in the guise of a lecturer in psychology, to study conditions there at first hand and report back on them to Cardinal Hinsley, whose student he had been at the English College in Rome. In 1937 Heenan became parish priest of St Stephen's, Manor Park. During

World War Two he established a wider reputation as an author and broadcaster. As Bishop of Leeds from 1951 he became a national figure through his appearances on television, and as Archbishop of Liverpool he was responsible for seeing that its long-deferred cathedral actually got built. As Archbishop of Westminster he was preoccupied with carrying through the reforms to Catholic practice decreed by the second Vatican Council.

Archbishop George Carey (1935 -) was born in Bow, brought up in Dagenham and, having failed his 11-plus examinations, attended Bifrons Secondary Modern School, which he left at fifteen without any qualifications. His future wife, Eileen, also from Dagenham, attended South East Essex Technical College and qualified as a nurse. Belated study brought Carey a doctorate and he went on to write fourteen books. After serving as Bishop of Bath and Wells from 1998, he became Archbishop of Canterbury in 1991 and announced his retirement in 2002.

104. *The prize-winning string orchestra at Westbury School in 1914.*

From Peace to War

A PROGRESSIVE TOWN

In 1902 Barking became one of the first local authorities to begin building council houses, with 85 in King Edward's Road. In 1903 Barking Council took over the functions of the School Board – Westbury School in Ripple Road opened the following year. Ripple School, another all-standard school, was opened in 1913 in bungalow-type buildings, one of the first in the country to be built as a one-storey complex.

Transport improvements were especially noteworthy. In 1903 the council inaugurated an electric tram service to Ilford and Beckton, extended to Loxford Bridge and the East Ham boundary in 1904-5. In 1904 a new Roding Bridge was opened on London Road. In 1902 an intermittent service of the District line reached Barking and when the line was fully electrified in 1908 the station was rebuilt. Increased road traffic created a need for an internal by-pass and in 1909-10 Abbey Road, an extension of Fisher Street, was built across former abbey lands, joining Heath Street to London Road. Land between this new road and the Roding was sold off for industrial develop-

ment. In 1909 River Road was also extended. By 1912 motor bus services connected Barking with central London.

Industry continued to expand. By 1906 Barking had some twenty manufacturers, half of them in chemicals of some sort. They were joined by Jonkoping & Vulcan's Abbey Match Works in the new Abbey Road (1908-10), Handley Page's aircraft factory at Creekmouth *(see below)* in 1909, the British Coalite Company in 1911 and, in 1913, the Cape Asbestos Company's factory in Harts Lane, which drew its raw material from South Africa. The latter enterprise would eventually give Barking one of Britain's highest death-rates from asbestosis. In 1912 the Barking Gas Company was absorbed by the Gas Light and Coke Company at Beckton, which henceforth became the town's supplier.

TAKING WING

Born at Cheltenham, Frederick Handley Page (1885-1962) was chief designer of an electrical company by the time he was twenty-one. Setting up as an aeronautical engineer in 1908, a year later, with a capital of ten thousand pounds, he

105. *Maypole dancing at North Street school in 1907.*

106. *A tram negotiating the bascule bridge which spanned the River Roding at the Barking Creek end. The bridge, built in 1903 to transport workers to Beckton Gas Works, was used by trams only though, as the picture shows, a man on a bicycle is taking advantage of the opportunity of the bridge being lowered. The bridge was demolished after the tram service was abandoned in 1929.*

107. Barking tram depot in Jenkins Lane in 1904.

108.   An undated press cutting referring to the death of a Barking asbestos worker, who had succumbed to asbestosis during his working life between the wars.

BARKING MAN'S DEATH FROM ASBESTOSIS.

AN OLD STANDING CASE.

An inquest was held at Hammersmith on Monday, on Henry Weiss, aged 53, of Biffron-st., Barking, whose death was believed to have been due to asbestosis.

Deceased, it was stated, worked at a Barking asbestos factory from 1918 to 1920. Afterwards he was taken ill, suffering from lung trouble, and had treatment in several hospitals.

Sir Bernard Spilsbury said that death was due to asbestosis, a new word, but one which had found a recognised position in the medical nomenclature.

A verdict of Accidental death was recorded.

opened Britain's first aircraft factory at Creekmouth and built his first experimental glider, tested from the top of a Barking dyke, and a four-winged quadruplane. In 1910 he produced a single-seat monoplane, *Bluebird*, followed by *Yellow Peril*, which was offered to the public at £275. In 1911 the Barking factory produced the EHP5, the first aircraft to fly over London.

Handley Page's eventual success as an aircraft maker was by no means assured as the improvements in design which he achieved in these early years were bought at the cost of crash-landings and, in 1912, a double fatality. In that year Handley Page relocated his manufacturing operations to Cricklewood.

HEALTH AND WELFARE

The experience of raising recruits for the second Boer War of 1899-1902 exposed the appalling medical condition of the nation's youth, only a third of which was judged fully fit for combat. The outcome was a campaign for 'National Efficiency', whose motives were as much strategic as humanitarian. Health provision, nutrition, physical exercise, housing and education all came

109. Production at Handley Page in 1911.

under scrutiny and it is against this background of concern that local conditions in Barking should be examined.

In terms of health, for Barking the new century began badly with an epidemic of smallpox in 1901-02. In 1903, however, Barking's Medical Officer of Health recorded with satisfaction that the death rate of babies under one year was 113 per thousand live births, markedly less than the national average for England and Wales of 132. Even more striking was the fact that only half a dozen years previously, in 1897, the local Barking rate had stood at 178. In 1902 Parliament had at last passed a Certification of Midwives Act which had driven unqualified practitioners out of business. It seems improbable, however, that the impact of this measure could in itself account for such a dramatic change in so short a time. Indeed, it took years to enforce the ban completely and a successful prosecution against an unregistered midwife was brought in Barking as late as 1911. Credit must therefore be due in some measure to the efforts of the MoH and his team, so perhaps a measure of self-congratulation was in order. In 1906 Barking's MoH, Dr Fenton, recommended the appointment of a 'Lady Inspector' to check on the progress of new-born babies – the forerunner of the modern Health Visitor. He believed

that the cheap alternative – visits by well-meaning volunteer 'Lady Helpers' from the middle classes was fraught with social hazards which might impede effective supervision and assistance. The following year the Notification of Births Act gave the MoH the right to be notified of all births within 36 hours, thus facilitating effective after-care. Barking was one of the first areas to adopt the provisions of the Act and in the same year appointed its first Lady Health Visitor. In 1908 an Infant Welfare Clinic was established, where mothers could bring their babies on a Tuesday afternoon to be weighed.

Such progressive action must be set against a background in which progress needed to be made. In 1911 10.8% of Barking's population lived more than two to a room, compared with a national average of 9.1%. In neighbouring Ilford, by contrast, the figure was 2.1%. Infant mortality, perhaps the most sensitive general indicator of welfare, in Barking was almost twice as high (117 per 1,000 live births) as in Ilford (69). Servant-keeping was more than twice as common in Ilford as in Barking. On the other hand in 1910-11 sewerage was extended to Creekmouth and by 1914 there were only sixteen houses in the entire borough which did not have access to a mains water supply.

110. *Barking Workhouse in East Street. Painting by A B Bamford, 1905. The building was later used as the first public library in Barking.*

MEMORY, HOLD THE DOOR

While Barking's bureaucrats were advancing the borough's modernisation, one of its humbler residents was undertaking a one-man crusade to preserve some record of its rapidly disappearing past "since the adoption of the Local Board, such is the alteration taken place in the Town, that an inhabitant who left the town thirty years ago would scarcely recognise it today." Between the 1890s and about 1910 William Holmes Frogley (1855-1924), the son of a Barking fishing captain, amassed almost five hundred foolscap pages of notes, sketches and ephemera into a hefty volume which not only remained unpublished but was, in effect, 'lost' until rediscovered in Colchester by County Archivist Dr F G Emmison in 1965. In 2002 the Borough published *Mr. Frogley's Barking: a First Selection* by Tony Clifford and Herbert Hope Lockwood, the editors characterising their effort as a combination of "illustrated guidebook to Victorian Barking and a gossip column about our ancestors". The latter include such distinct personalities as Blind Scotcher, the harpist, and William Holmes, Frogley's own revered uncle, "expert bricklayer, builder, Auc-

tioneer, Architect, Publican". Clifford and Lockwood not only rescued Frogley from undeserved obscurity but also emphasised the value of his work to family, as well as local, historians, containing as it does references to some 3,000 local inhabitants and 1,400 minor place names.

There is an arm-tugging quality to Frogley's idiosyncratic prose style, blending exposition with reminiscence and occasional speculation. A grocer-turned-estate agent, he would have been especially aware of changes in the use and ownership of local properties and businesses. Although painstaking in recording information, Frogley was also judgmental, commenting on individual cases of bankruptcy and suicide, observing of one man that his employees thought him a bully, of another that he drank very heavily and of a third that the congregation of 'Brethren' had ostracised him for marrying his late wife's sister. Frogley deplored the passing of the traditional Barking Fair and recorded with approval how, after its passing, his uncle and namesake, William Holmes, would give out free Ginger Bread to customers on the days when the fair had formerly been held. He also mourned the disap-

pearance of such traditional sources of employment as the saw-pit and the rope-walk and the collapse of commerce in Heath Street; the town's most bustling thoroughfare during the fishing boom, it had fallen to "a very dilapidated and forsaken condition". The development of industrial premises along Hart Street had likewise reduced it "from a decent residential place to ... a slum." Like many looking back on youth Frogley saw society as having gone to the dogs:

" ... Barking during that period was worth living in. I cannot remember any case of extreme poverty, there seemed work for all ... There is no comparison so far as the general health – strength – comfort – contentment and social condition of the inhabitants was concerned that prevailed in 1860 and later with what prevails now in 1900. Everyone knew and assisted each other then - now I am afraid to express what I think."

Frogley illustrated his handwritten manuscript

111. 'Blind Scotcher', the harpist, depicted in Frogley's manuscript of memories of Barking.

112. The Servants' Hall at Eastbury House, painted by A B Bamford.

113. *Upney Lane c.1910.*

114. *East Street c.1905. On the corner to the left is the Bull public house.*

volume with colour-washed plans of estates and sketches of prominent buildings, many of which are the only surviving representations of landmarks long vanished.

A far more accomplished visual record was produced by professional art teacher Alan Bennett Bamford (1857-1939). Born in Romford and based mainly in Chelmsford, Bamford made hundreds of sketches and watercolours of Essex subjects. His pictures of Barking include the Elizabethan Courthouse, the Curfew Tower, Barking Workhouse, Wellington Mill, St Margaret's church and the Servants' Hall, Eastbury Manor House.

EASTBURY AT RISK

Eastbury House came close to being pulled down in the 1830s. Local antiquarian and schoolmaster Edward Sage, who gathered an important collection of manuscripts and materials relating to the history of Barking, managed to persuade Eastbury's then owner, Wasey Sterry, that the building was of historical and architectural importance. Sterry, however, greatly dismayed Sage in 1841 by modernizing the interior "in a cockneyfied manner" and converting much of the building into stables, granaries and coach houses. Sterry then died the following year, insane.

Occupied by farmers thereafter Eastbury once more deteriorated. Visiting it in 1861 D W Coller, author of *The People's History of Essex*, found "long galleries wreathed with cobwebs and half-filled with lumber - large apartments converted into lofts for hay, corn and harnesses, with remnants of ancient frescoes here and there to be traced on the walls - sad memorials of their faded grandeur."

When the surrounding estate was being broken up for building on in 1913 Eastbury House once again came under threat of demolition. The Society for the Protection of Ancient Buildings energetically raised the funds necessary for its salvation. The London Survey Committee researched and published a learned monograph outlining the history of the structure and its inhabitants. As a result of these efforts Eastbury House was bought by the National Trust.

WORLD WAR I – LOCAL HERO

Sergeant J H C Drain (1895-1975) of the 37th Battery, Royal Field Artillery won the Victoria Cross, within the first month of the war, on 26 August 1914. The incident for which he was honoured took place at Le Cateau, where the captain of his battery was trying to recapture two

115. Barking Park c.1905.

116 and 117.   *Transition at the heart of Barking. The Paddock, an 18th-century house pictured above, stood at the junction of Ripple Road and East Street, now the site of Boots the chemist. According to Frogley, it was built by Roger Vaughan, a brandy merchant. At the time of this photograph it was owned by Thomas Glenny who retired from the family brewery business in Linton Road in 1907. In about 1911 Cllr Arthur Blake built a furnishing and ironmongery store, as below, on the site – his shop became known as 'Blake's Corner'.*

118. The Town Quay in 1906.

guns. Job Drain, then a driver and just eighteen years of age, volunteered with another driver, to assist and together they did manage to recover one of the guns, despite being under heavy infantry and artillery fire from the rapidly advancing enemy only a hundred yards away. All three men were awarded the VC. The gun in question is now on display in the Imperial War Museum. At the time Drain's portrait was portrayed on a cigarette card and decades later military artist Terence Cuneo immortalised 'Saving the Guns at Le Cateau' in a dramatic painting. Job Drain subsequently attended the Buckingham Palace Garden Party given for holders of the VC in 1920, was a member of the VC Honour Guard for the burial of the Unknown warrior in November of that same year and took part in the review held in 1956 to mark the centenary of the inauguration of the award.

Born in Barking, Drain also died in Barking and is buried in Rippleside cemetery.

LEST WE FORGET

Barking's main war memorial, unveiled in Barking Park in 1922, bore the names of some 820 dead. Over succeeding decades, however, many of the names became illegible. Even more regrettably the original master record of the names was destroyed by enemy action in the Second World War. Following a public appeal for information to reconstitute the memorial list it was rededicated in August 2001. There is another outdoor memorial at Rippleside Cemetery as well as memorials in the church of SS Mary and Ethelburga (63 names), Barking Baptist Tabernacle (19 names) and Barking United Reformed Church (8 names). The memorial in St Margaret's parish church, records the names of Territorials of D (Barking) Company of the 4th Battalion of the Essex Regiment recalled to the colours at the outbreak of war and subsequently killed in action – a dozen private soldiers, three lance-corporals, two lieutenants, a sergeant-major and no less than seven sergeants. St Margaret's Church of England school holds a roll of honour bearing the names of 66 former pupils.

Remaking Barking

For Barking the inter-war period would witness not only a further massive expansion of population to out-do even that of the 1890s but also the disappearance of further heritage properties and distinctive landscape features. In 1923 the Elizabethan Court House was demolished against representations from the Committee of the Survey of London, the Essex Archaeological Society, the Society for the Protection of Ancient Buildings, the British Archaeological Association and the Gilbert White Fellowship. The well-preserved woodwork was set aside as a concession to the critics. Some was eventually used to make doors for the new Town Hall. The restored royal coat of arms can be seen in Court No. I at the Magistrates Court. As for the rest .... This act of destruction continued to rankle with the local opponents who had mobilised such imposing

supporters of their cause. When, over a decade later, on the occasion of a rain-sodden formal visit by the British Archaeological Society to view the site of the Abbey, the Mayor made an ill-judged attempt to insert a defence of the demolition of the Court House into his official words of welcome, he was openly rebuked by local notable Robert Hewett.

In 1935 Bridge Street and the dilapidated sixteenth-century market buildings in Back Lane were finally pulled down. Cecil House and Northbury House went in 1936, Manor (Jenkins) Farm in 1937. The wholesale redevelopment of the Broadway in the mid-1930s took with it the Queens' Head among many other older structures. Axe Street received similar treatment.

Offsetting the losses were such new civic amenities as the Central Library in Ripple Road, a museum in Eastbury House *(see below)* and a new Fire Station in Alfred's Way.

The area already had one newspaper, *The Barking Advertiser,* which had been founded as long ago as 1888. Roy Greenslade, writing in 2001,

119. The demolition of the Elizabethan Market House/Courthouse in 1923.

commended the paper as "The glue that held the community together". The community's sense of itself was further strengthened by the establishment of *The Barking and Dagenham Post* in 1923 and the foundation of the Barking and District Archaeological Society in 1934.

One Victorian legacy whose passing was not to be regretted was overcrowded housing. The 1921 census revealed that Barking's population of 35,523 was accommodated in 6,770 inhabited houses: 11.5% lived more than two persons to a room, compared with just 3.1% in adjacent Ilford, where there was not only an average of 5.75 rooms per dwelling, compared with Barking's 4.72, but the number of persons per family averaged only 3.98 compared with Barking's 4.64. In 1931 Barking still had 6.37% of its households living more than two to a room compared with 1.69% in Ilford

Between 1918 and 1938 Barking itself as a local authority built 992 new houses and a further 552 to replace cleared slums. But these efforts, worthy as they were, were totally overshadowed by the unprecedented scheme undertaken by the London County Council.

120 and 121. Slums in Axe Street (above) and in Back Lane in 1932 and 1933 respectively.

THE BUILDING OF BECONTREE

When it was built Becontree was the world's biggest council estate. As the LCC's own architect observed in 1920 "the proposal to convert a tract of land, three thousand acres in extent, at present covered chiefly with market gardens, into a township with a population of 120,000 is something altogether unparalleled in the history of housing."

Becontree represented a major attempt to redeem the rash pledge of wartime premier David Lloyd George that ex-servicemen should return to 'homes fit for heroes'. Walter Long, president of the Local Government Board, regarded the commitment as the redemption of a moral obligation to those who had endured the horrors of the Western Front: "To let them come home from horrible, water-logged trenches to something little better than a pigsty here would, indeed, be criminal ... and a negation of all we have said during the war, that we can never repay those men for what they have done for us." Others, more cynically, saw government-subsidised housing as "the antidote to Bolshevism."

Whatever the motivation, the 'cottage-style' residences of Becontree were intended to be superior to the former general run of working-class housing in terms of spaciousness, fittings and standards of construction. Gas and electricity supplies, front and back gardens, inside lavatories and fitted baths were all to be standard features. As if in acknowledgment of the superiority of this provision tenants were expected to observe strict guidelines in terms of family behaviour and 'self-reliance'. Windows, for example, were to be washed once a week, an onerous chore, considering that they invariably consisted of small panes. In the detailed handbook of regulations presented to each new householder specific attention was directed to the regular maintenance of chimneys, drains and even door-hinges.

Starting in 1921 over 25,000 houses were built within the parish boundaries of Dagenham, Barking and Ilford. The architect was G. Topham Forrest, who also designed Chelsea Bridge. Forrest was among a number of British architects intrigued by the American 'Garden City' concept

122. An aerial view of part of Becontree, just outside the Barking borders. Looking east, it shows Valence Circus bisected by Aylmer Road. Valence Wood Road and Valence Park are to the left.

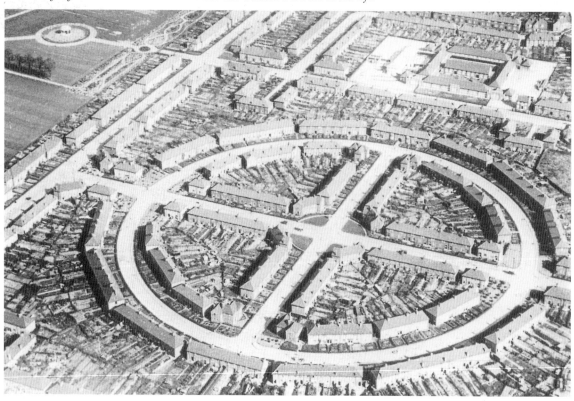

123. *Captain Amies, land agent during the formation of the Becontree Estate in the 1920s, outside Gale Street Farm, where he lived. Also shown are his daughter and his son Hardy, in later life to be a famous fashion designer.*

and in 1923 contributed an article on the post-war reconstruction of the ancient Belgian city of Ypres to the Journal of the Royal Institute of British Architects.

Hampered initially by shortages of men and materials, the Becontree programme was soon also faced by rising costs. The £750 initially estimated as the construction cost per house rose to £1,150, although it would later fall back dramatically to nearer £400. To speed the acquisition of land the LCC installed its own resident agent and valuer in a farmhouse on Gale Street, Captain H W Amies, father of future royal fashion designer, Hardy Amies, who commuted from there to school in Brentwood.

Once building operations achieved momentum they employed some six thousand craftsmen and labourers and required the delivery of over 2,500 tons of materials daily. Gravel and sand were excavated locally but most of what was needed came via two specially-constructed light railways. With almost a hundred houses being completed

weekly, the influx of newcomers reached a peak in 1928-9, when, in that single period, it exceeded the entire population of Chelmsford.

Most newcomers delighted in the fresh air and freedom from overcrowding but others missed the street-life of the East End from which over half of them had come. Shops were ranked in imposing 'parades', rather than at the corner of the street. There were no markets or stalls, though itinerant traders selling from carts proved popular with local inhabitants, if not with the authorities. The few pubs permitted were cavernous and characterless – one for every ten thousand inhabitants, compared to one to six hundred in Bethnal Green. The planners had envisaged "a township more or less complete in itself" but that was not what actually materialised. The incomers recorded their own verdict. In the first ten years a third moved away voluntarily. A preliminary study of this new community, by then as populous as Norwich or Blackburn, was conducted in 1934 by the Pilgrim Trust. Prime Minister Stanley

124. *A special light railway was constructed to carry building material from the Thames to the Becontree Estate while it was being built. It crossed the two arms of the London-Southend railway and ended up in sidings at Chadwell Heath. The middle of Valence Avenue, now a stretch of grass, was still a railway line until 1934.*

Baldwin, who was also the Trust's chairman, noted regretfully "I cannot help hoping that the restriction of 'housing' to the provision of houses alone may be reconsidered."

There were many other lessons to be learned from the construction of "the first new town in England". The site's lack of striking natural features made it difficult to create pleasing perspectives. Although designers produced 91 house types, including varieties built with concrete panels or weather-boarding, the vast majority were built of the same materials, at the same height and with little detailing to differentiate them. The characteristic cul-de-sacs, immediately christened 'banjos' by the residents, were a success, saving on road construction costs, cutting down through-traffic and fostering sociability, but the major boulevards, with 32 foot central reservations set aside for future tramways which never materialised, proved depressing.

Although the largest tranche of homes and the first to be put up were in Dagenham, a third of the scheme, amounting to 7,332 houses by 1934, lay in Barking. In a partial effort to create a mixed rather than a one-class community, some of these were offered for sale into private ownership, rather than for occupation by rent-paying council tenants. The Longbridge estate offered 4-bed-room houses with a garage for £965, deposit £75 pounds. As the Barking part was built rather later Barking as an authority had more time to respond to the exceptional new demands which would be created for public amenities and services.

RESPONSES

The construction of the Becontree estate necessitated a substantial expansion in locally provided services, including health, transport and leisure.

A local midwifery service had already been established in 1919. The ending of the war reunited millions of couples long separated and a post-war 'baby boom' might reasonably have been expected in such circumstances, regardless of other changes planned for the area. Becontree boosted demand still further, having a birth-rate twice the national average. Further specialist provision was made with the opening of Upney Maternity Pavilion in 1936. An orthopaedic aftercare service was established in 1925 and

125. *Construction of the Scrattons Farm Estate, south of Ripple Road. This estate, built by Barking Council in the late 1930s, was on an isolated site on marshy land, surrounded by fields and irrigation ditches down to the Thames. Though consisting only of 2-storey houses, it was referred to by non-residents as 'Hollywood', which is testament to the level of expectations of council tenants at that time.*

126. *The Capitol Cinema opened on 21 October 1929, seating 1,266. It was designed by J. Aldridge. It closed on 12 December 1959, and the building was used by Marks & Spencer as an extension to their store.*

Barking Hospital opened in 1932. In 1938 a specialist Ear, Nose and Throat service became available and a Chiropody Clinic was established.

Improved transport was also needed to enable Becontree residents to get to work and housewives the occasional chance to relieve their isolation by means of a shopping expedition or a visit to relatives. Barking's new bus garage was opened in 1924 and in the same year the construction of a Barking by-pass was commenced, to be completed by 1928. In 1929 Barking trams were leased to East Ham and Ilford councils and between 1936 and 1940 they were replaced by trolleybuses. In 1932 the District line, rather late for the earlier residents of the Becontree estate, was extended from Barking to Upminster. From 1936 the Metropolitan Line extended services to Barking during peak hours and in 1937 London Road was extended to join Ripple Road.

The cinema reached the peak of its popularity in the 1930s. Younger, urban, working-class females constituted the most loyal core of the national audience and were well represented on the Becontree estate. Local cinema-goers heading for Barking could patronise the Capitol, Rialto, Electric or Bioscope.

From 1931 hardier souls could have recourse to the new open-air swimming pool in Barking Park. Although the Becontree planners did consciously set aside large 'sylvan belts' for recreational use, the provision of actual amenities could not be regarded as generous. Becontree's planners did provide "healthy and moral surroundings" but little in the way of fun.

What Becontree residents did get, however, was a first-class library service, created by the redoubtable J G O'Leary (died 1985), as he himself put it: "without any exterior aid, government grant, or the exercise of benevolence and in a place with no advantages." An expert on recusant history, O'Leary in 1950 was to rediscover the original manuscript of Lethieullier's *History of Barking* in the Hulse collection at Breamore House in Hampshire, where it was thought to have been destroyed by fire in 1857. His crowning achievement, however, was to bring the fine collection of Fanshawe family portraits to their ancestral property, Valence House.

127. *Construction of the Rio Cinema opposite Barking Station in 1935. It later became the Odeon and most recently the site is being redeveloped. The cinema, designed by George Coles and seating 2,200, opened on 17 August 1935. In 1995, by then a 6-screen complex, it was the only cinema left in Barking.*

128. *The Bioscope Cinema in the Broadway, just before demolition in the late 1940s. It opened c.1914, but could seat only 650.*

129. *A sign of Barking's acceptance by the chain stores, was the building of a Burton's shop in East Street. This picture, taken in 1931, also shows the trolleybus wires that visually cluttered the streets at the time.*

EDUCATION

No need was more pressing than educational provision. Barking had already opened a special school in 1920. In 1922 Essex County Council established Barking Abbey as one of Britain's earliest co-educational grammar schools. Located just inside Ilford, it was nevertheless intended primarily to serve the needs of Barking. The school's development was to be dominated by its dynamic, if domineering, head Col. Ernest Achey Loftus CBE., TD, DL, MA, Sc., LCP., FRGS, FSA (1884-1987), a fervent subscriber to the school motto, *Laborare et Servire,* and a strict disciplinarian in its accomplishment. A Yorkshireman, Loftus had already had over twenty years teaching experience when he was appointed as Barking Abbey's first head. After a second career break with the army, Loftus retired in 1949 only to launch himself on yet another career as an education officer in Africa in 1953, finally retiring in 1975. He can be found in the *Guinness Book of Records* under Most Durable Teachers and again under Longest Diary. His ashes were interred in the grounds of the Abbey.

As well as aiming at high academic standards Barking Abbey also encouraged pupils to excel outside the classroom. Ju-jitsu was offered as a sport for both boys and girls in the 1930s. A member of staff, Elsie Harris, was captain of the Welsh hockey team and an international for thirteen years. Distinguished alumni include the educationist Royston Lambert and the composer Robert Layton.

Additional local provision was made in 1926 with the opening of Park Selective Central School in Rosslyn Road and a new Roman Catholic elementary school St Joseph's, opened in Linton Road in 1927. In the same year St Ethelburga's Catholic school was reorganised for seniors.

The building of the Barking phase of the Becontree estate between 1930 and 1934 added ten thousand children to the borough's school population. Between 1930 and the outbreak of war Barking education Committee rebuilt the Central School, reorganised Gascoigne, Northbury, Westbury and Ripple schools and added no less than nine more new ones.

In 1936 South East Essex Technical College and School of Art was opened in Longbridge Road "to cultivate an interest in the wider problems of modern industry rather than in the technical difficulties of particular processes." Alumni have included the Trinidadian film star Edric Connor (1913-68), the painter and designer Edward Pond (1929-) and the potter Alan Spencer Green (1932-).

130. *The formidable Colonel Loftus in his study at Barking Abbey School. Date unknown.*

131. *Bifrons School, from a drawing made in 1932.*

132. *The Domestic Science room at Cambell Senior School, in the 1930s.*

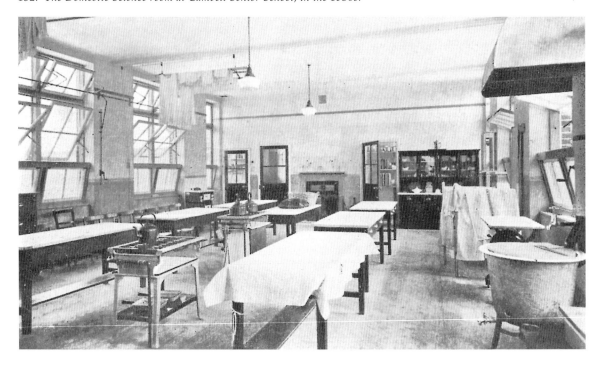

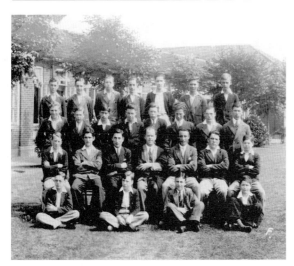

133. *A Barking Abbey boys' form in 1932.*

INDUSTRY AND EMPLOYMENT

The Barking Manufacturers' Association was founded in 1919 and was to prove a more effective body in promoting the area's industries and attracting inward investment than many similar institutions. In particular when the depression was at its worst, in 1931, it took positive action by organizing an industrial exhibition to showcase the range of the borough's industrial capacity.

By 1921 Barking's leading local industries were the manufacture of matches (530 workers), rubber and rubber goods (510), chemicals (454) and associated products, such as ink and gum. More than half the occupied population, 8,592 residents, worked outside Barking itself, half in central London and a substantial proportion of the rest in West Ham.

A new industrial estate was built with a Thames frontage and in 1922 the historic Quayside millhouse was demolished to clear its site for more productive use. In 1926 another local landmark, Wellington Mill, fell to the wreckers. Incoming new businesses helped to diversify the local industrial base still further. P.C. Henderson, manufacturers of sliding doors, established a works in Barking in 1921. A welcome indicator of the promise of new technologies was the opening of the radio factory of A F Bulgin and Co. in 1923. New leisure-related markets were represented by Dicky Bird Ltd., manufacturers of crackers, novelties and ice-cream. In 1927 the Abbey Match Works, taken over by J J Masters in 1919, became part of the British Match Corporation Ltd. Local construction firm Sanders and Foster built Barking's new bus garage, a new

134. *The Dicky Bird ice cream factory on the Barking By-pass, decorated and the staff presented to mark the coronation of George VI in May 1937.*

135. *The tin box factory at the plant of Gross, Sherwood and Heald Ltd, Barking, 1910.*

grandstand at Lord's cricket ground, Barking's Capitol cinema and the Mayfair cinema at Whalebone Lane South.

In retrospect it seems astonishing that the planning for such a vast venture as the Becontree estate should have contained no explicit steps for the provision of local employment opportunities. As it happened the decision of the Ford Motor Company to take advantage of deep water access to a Thames-side location by building a motor works at Dagenham in 1929-31 was, to say the least, fortuitous. Amazingly Ford workers relocating from Manchester were initially declared ineligible for accommodation on the Becontree estate.

Another major new source of employment was the opening of a massive new power station at Creekmouth in 1925 *(see below)*.

Inter-war observers of Britain's social scene stressed the disparity between the deprivations current in the 'distressed areas' of the North, Scotland and Wales and the relative prosperity of the Midlands and South East. Yet even in the

latter there were internal disparities which condemned many to lives of hardship. In Barking in 1929 11.4 % of households were living in poverty with a weekly income of two pounds or less, 37.4% were on two to three pounds, 39.1 % were on three to five pounds and only 12.15 %, just under one in eight, could count on over five pounds.

THE POWER STATION

"... this giant edifice from which such copious energy flows".

The opening of Barking Power House at Creekmouth by King George V took place on 19 May 1925. In the foreword to the lavishly-illustrated souvenir book produced to mark the occasion Sir Harry Renwick, the Chairman and Managing Director of the County of London Electric Supply Co. Ltd, proclaimed that its inauguration marked "the opening of a new era: it marks the culmination, in a word, of the greatest step yet taken for London and district in the supply of electrical power ...".

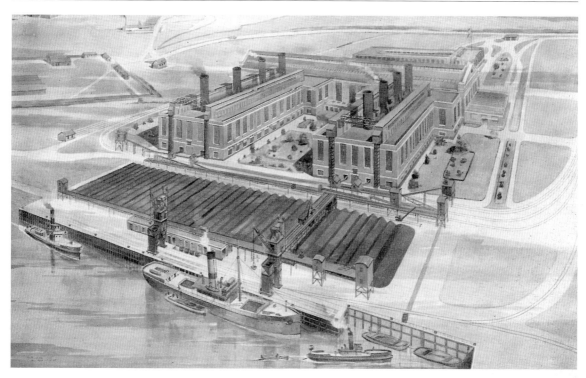

136. A perspective view of the proposed first section of Barking Power Station.

When electricity supply first became available in the 1880s it was conceived as a modern convenience to be utilized for lighting. Broader applications as a source of power for industry and transport remained largely unsuspected. Parliament favoured the provision of supply on a purely local basis for each community, with the option of compulsory purchase by the local authority. Electricity companies were explicitly forbidden to associate with one another. Over succeeding decades it became apparent that this policy led to the erection of too many small and relatively inefficient generating stations, frustrating the possibility of achieving economies of scale, with corresponding reductions in cost, at the very time that demand for energy was escalating remorselessly.

In 1919 a new Electricity Supply Act reversed the previous policy. Interestingly responsibility for supervision of the industry passed from the Board of Trade to the Minister of Transport, who was empowered to rationalise supply by closing down old and inadequate stations, promote co-operation between suppliers and promote the construction of new stations. The construction of Barking's giant Powerhouse was the outcome of

this reappraisal of national policy. Between December 1919 and March 1924 Britain's generating capacity expanded over 91%, from 3,080,000 horse-power to 5,900,000 horse-power. This was accompanied by a 17% increase in fuel efficiency in 1921-3. Although the forward-looking County of London Electricity Supply Company had obtained authority in principle to construct the Barking station as long ago as 1913 the outbreak of the Great War and the opposition of affected interests delayed the final go-ahead until June 1922. Construction began in January 1923 and employed ten thousand men, thus easing what was already openly recognised as "the misery of unemployment". Renwick forcefully argued that the new facility would not only enable supply to be enhanced at reduced cost, it would also encourage "the transfer of factories from congested districts to more healthy neighbourhoods." The prospect of electricity replacing gas for cooking and heating in the home opened up further enticing vistas.

A self-consciously progressive employer, the County of London Company, with over a thousand staff encouraged employees to develop clubs for billiards, bowls, chess, cricket, football, rifle

137. *View from the river of Barking Power Station, as it was intended to be. This was published in a booklet produced to mark the opening of the first stage on 19 May 1925.*

138. *From the same booklet, a sketch showing the coal conveyor and boiler house.*

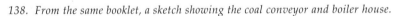

shooting, tennis and the new-fangled 'wireless'. Dances, concerts and whist drives were organised in the winter months. There was also a horticultural society, a staff magazine and a superannuation fund. The Company was particularly proud that over four hundred employees had served in the Great War, their positions being kept open for them and allowances paid to their families. Moreover "at the present time the Company has over twelve per cent of disabled men on its staff – which compares very favourably with the five per cent necessary to secure qualification for the King's Roll of Honour."

The building was erected on what was characterised as "a desolate spot... acres of unfertile, unpleasing marshy lands" – not the medieval appreciation of a rich grazing property. It occupied a site of a hundred acres with a river frontage of 2,100 feet. What was created was claimed to be "the greatest source of electric power - certainly in the Empire, if not in the world." There was an additional three hundred acres "with river and railway facilities ... levelled preparatory to being let as required for the erection of factories needing electric power, particularly for such purposes as electric furnaces, electro-metallurgical manufactures, chemical processes and others needing unlimited energy at the lowest possible rates." The Company's guiding vision was revealed in its claim that "With such a programme no great effort of imagination ... is needed to see, in the mind's eye, a second Trafford Park here within a few years." In keeping with its "usual forward policy" the Company pledged to draw on its reserves, in excess of three million pounds, to help finance the erection of factories.

The actual work of construction was preceded by site preparation entrusted to a team of civil engineers "who, with the competence and unconcern with which civil engineers can alter a landscape, took charge; diverted drainage outfalls; constructed new ones; made roads; and prepared foundations in a manner and on a scale worthy of an ode by Kipling." To create a firm base 300,000 tons of earth and rubbish were removed by diggers, then 3,000 reinforced concrete piles, weighing five tons each, were driven down to a minimum depth of forty feet. On this base were erected 4,000 tons of steel and 2,500,000 bricks to house plant and machinery weighing 35,000 tons. The building itself was, characteristically for the period, likened to "a four-funnelled liner". To carry electricity to south London a tunnel half

a mile long was driven under the Thames. The Rotherhithe Tunnel was also cabled to ensure a back-up supply. Master-minding the entire project was the engineering design consultancy of Merz and McLellan. Charles Hesterman Merz (1874-1940) was a Geordie of German descent and Quaker upbringing. By the time he was in his twenties his expertise in electrical engineering had put him in charge of Cork's electricity supply. There he met William McClellan, who became his partner until his death in 1934. Their business involved contracts in markets as distant as America, Australia and Argentina. It was Merz as chairman of the electric power supply subcommittee of the wartime coal conservation committee who formulated the concept of a 'national grid'. He also served as first director of the Admiralty's Department of Experiment and Research. Merz was to give distinguished service to the Institution of Electrical Engineers and the Royal Institution but refused all public honours for his many services to government. Merz and both his children were to be killed by a direct hit on his Kensington home during the blitz of 1940.

The purely architectural aspects of the project were devolved to the firm recently established by Sir Alexander Gibb (1872-1958). Gibb came from a four-generation dynasty of engineers and could number among his forebears pupils of Rennie and Telford. His own achievements included the Whitechapel to Bow section of the Metropolitan railway and the Rosyth naval base. Later he would design the Guinness brewery at Park Royal and the prefabricated Mulberry harbour system used to support the D-day landings in Normandy.

The recently appointed general manager of the County of London Company at the time of the opening of the Barking Powerhouse was a Scot, Archibald Page (1875-1949), who would be knighted in 1930 for his work in creating the National Grid.

The king only opened phase one of the project, in fact in terms of capacity, only half of phase one, which was intended to produce 250,000 horsepower.

But the technology it embraced represented a revolution in working procedures:

"Here are no mounds of loose coal, no grimy overworked stokers shovelling coal eternally into gaping furnace doors which, no sooner are they closed, gape again insatiably ... In fact, the word 'boilers' seems entirely impertinent ... these lofty erections of iron and steel, towering into gleams of daylight near the roof, are steam generators ...

139. *Another view of the proposed Barking Power Station, illustrated in 1925.*

And the 'stokers' are mechanical ... worthy of Dante's pen." These in turn were expected to produce "cleaner factories and workshops, the gradual elimination from factory areas of the smoke and grime which used to be considered inevitable accomplishments of manufacturing districts and contented bodies of workers in cleanly surroundings ...".

LOOKING AHEAD

At the depth of the inter-war depression Barking UDC created a Development Committee to boost investment and employment in the locality. Barking's local boosters believed they were batting from a strong position: "power costs are low; waterfront industrial sites are plentiful and relatively cheap; there is direct road and rail communication with London and Tilbury docks; labour is available in abundance; the building regulations allow great freedom in regard to factory construction and are generally free from irritating restrictions." The local skills profile was especially impressive with "over five hundred classifications ... registered at the Local Employment Exchange."

As a result of these advantages Barking already had a highly diversified manufacturing sector producing "Rubber Flooring, Motor Tyres, Rubber Boots, Gloves, Clogs, Sliding Door Gear, Runways, Baths, Stoves, Rainwater Goods, Matches, Radio Components, Paint, Varnish, Distempers, Coke, Drugs, Acids, Tar, Bitumen, Chemicals, Joinery, Office Furniture, Office Appliances, Iron Drums, Tin Containers, Life Belts, Life Saving Apparatus, Concrete Partition Blocks, Shellac, Scientific Instruments, Compasses, Barometers, Asbestos Goods, Iron and Metal Castings." Other local specialist firms dealt with "Structural Steelwork, Wood Block Paving and Flooring, Decorative and Plain Panelling, Concrete Fireproof Flooring, Mechanical Engineering and Building."

THE PAGEANT

Barking finally achieved borough status in 1931 and decided to mark this municipal milestone with a 'Charter Pageant', both as a means of promoting the borough to outsiders and of involving newcomers to the area to foster a sense of identification with the community. When it came to the latter no opportunities were lost. The biggest pageant scene involved a cast of over three hundred. Its firmly historical theme represented perhaps an unspoken desire to reaffirm

140. *The new borough's coat-of-arms. The motto,* Dei Gratia Sumus Quod Sumus *means By the Grace of God we are what we are.*

continuity and belonging at a time of rapid social change and economic uncertainty. The effort that went into the enterprise was prodigious. Every one of the eleven scenes presented had its own separate organising committee. Even the three smallest ones had six members, consisting of chairman, secretary, stage manager, deputy stage manager, marshal and property master. The largest had thirteen members. Three committees even found it necessary to appoint their own treasurer.

Complementing the scene committees was a further battery of functional committees. The largest were the Designs and Costumes Committee with 61 members and the Performers Committee with 54. There was also a Historical Committee, Reception Committee, Amphitheatre Committee, Ticket Committee, Exhibition Committee and an Arrangements Committee as well as further committees for Publicity, Properties, Music and Dancing, Transport, Finance, Illuminations and Street Decorations, Street Processions, Shop Displays and Cinematography.

Multiple office-holding and memberships provide a glimpse of the local power elite in action. The Finance and Concessions Committees were entirely in the hands of councillors. Colonel Loftus, ubiquitous headmaster of Barking Abbey school, was chairman of two scene committees and a member of the Historical, Performers, Properties and Publicity Committees. He also wrote eight of the eleven scenes of the pageant. Councillor Howe, the only other chairman of two scene committees, was also chairman of the Performers

141. *A splendidly flamboyant Frank Lascelles, 'Master' of the Barking Pageant of 1931, clutching a palette and regarding a clematis. One wonders how he got on with Colonel Loftus.*

Committee and a member of the Finance Committee and the Illuminations and Street Decorations Committee. Councillor Sanders chaired the Exhibition, Publicity and Concessions Committees and was a member of the Amphitheatre and Finance Committees. Clearly an organisation man, however, he eschewed service on the scene committees. Councillor Whiting chaired the Arrangements Committee and was a member of no less than seven others. Councillor Graham, chairman of the Council, limited himself to chairing two committees and sat on six others, while his wife was secretary of the Designs and Costumes Committee. Councillor Garland chaired a scene committee and the Ticket Committee and sat on three others – and played Charles I.

Nor was the urge to office an entirely male prerogative. Mrs B E Jackson, apart from chairing the Designs and Costumes Committee, sat on four others. Mrs Sheffield ('Lady Leicester') chaired the Historical Committee and sat on four others. Between them three generations of the Glenny family chaired a scene committee and sat

142. *The procession in 1931 to celebrate the incorporation of Barking as a borough.*

on four other committees. Four members of the Hewett family were on committees, one on two and another on three. Perhaps surprisingly the Town Clerk, Mr Jewers, contented himself with serving as secretary to the Reception and Arrangements Committees, from which strategic positions he could doubtless observe with some detachment the labours of the rest. More than a decade after the ending of the Great War not only did Col. Loftus retain his military title but so did five Captains and Stage Manager Sergeant-Major (for thespian purposes Centurion) Brettingham.

Despite this plethora of eager volunteers the organisers felt the need to appoint a 'Master of the Pageant' to ensure that their efforts achieved the correct artistic tone. The appointment fell to Frank Lascelles (1875-1934), who was about as well qualified a candidate as it was possible to find. A lifelong bachelor and close friend of Ivor Novello, Lascelles (born Stevens) had been a star of the Oxford University Dramatic Society but left the Varsity without a degree. Undaunted, he acted under Sir Herbert Beerbohm Tree, changed

his name and assumed the title of Lord of the Manor of Sibthorp Gower, the Cotswolds village of his birth, where he converted a barn into a pseudo-medieval castle. Starting with a pageant at Oxford, which turned into a near riot, Lascelles swiftly created a career for himself by staging the Canadian Tercentenary pageant in 1908, the Pageant of London for George V's coronation in 1910, the Coronation Durbar in India the following year and, as a crowning glory, the Pageant of Empire at the Crystal Palace in 1924, with 15,000 participants. For Barking Lascelles obligingly posed for an appropriately aesthetic photographic portrait, draped in an artist's robe and clutching a painterly palate while thoughtfully regarding a clematis. Lascelles, intriguingly, sat only on the Cinematograph Committee. Barking was one of his last triumphs, as the depression choked off the sort of funds needed for such extravagances. His health failed tragically with his luck. The socialite who had once lorded it over an Oxfordshire village in baronial style died in poverty in a bed-sit in Brighton.

The casting of the various scenes for the pageant reveals much about Barking's associational life. Scene I, The Romans at Uphall Camp, fell to members of the Territorial units, Ex-service Men's Association and the Barking branch of the Old Contemptibles. The Foundation and Dissolution of Barking Abbey was assigned to the local Roman Catholic community and the funeral of Bishop Erkenwald to the local branch of Toc H. The boys of Barking Abbey school were allowed to rampage as Vikings. Other scenes were assigned to members of the Free Churches, the Church of England, the Women's Citizens League supported by local teachers and the local bowling Clubs ('King Charles I plays a game of bowls at Barking'). The climactic scene – The Great Barking Fair A.D. 1746 – had an appropriately catch-all cast – members of the Conservative Association, the Barking Hospital Committee, the Hospital Women's Linen Guild and the Barking Rowing and Athletic Club.

The celebrations stretched over eleven days. A funfair and Industrial Exhibition, opened on 1 October, were graced by the presence of actress Anna Neagle. Pageant rehearsals took up the next two days. On 5 October Prince George came to inspect a guard of honour, plant the first tree in Exhibition Avenue, watch the first performance of the pageant and hand over the actual Charter of Incorporation. A Guards band was in attendance and the day closed with fireworks. The Lord Mayor of London came the following day in full pomp, accompanied by his Swordbearer. Two days later the honoured guest was gas supply supremo Sir David Milne-Watson, accompanied by Beckton's own band. Two days after him the guest was the socialist socialite, the Countess of Warwick. Watched by a crowd of 50,000 on Sunday 11 October a procession wound through the town as part of the first civic church service.

After the Second World War Barking settled for a conventional carnival.

143. *The opening of Eastbury House as a Barking museum in 1935.*

144. The north elevation of Eastbury House, a drawing published in 1917..

A MUSEUM FOR BARKING

Eastbury House was opened as a museum for Barking on 4 December 1935 by the Earl of Crawford and Balcarres, a Fellow of the Society of Antiquaries.

The building, by then a National Trust property, had been repaired rather than restored by architect William Weir. More than a thousand exhibits of historical or artistic importance had been assembled, as gifts or loans, from over a hundred individual and institutional donors and lenders, ranging from the king to Col. Loftus, from the Town Council of Southampton to the English Folk Dance and Song Society. There were loans from museums or galleries in Bolton, Bury St. Edmund's, Colchester, Ipswich, Manchester, Northampton and Saffron Walden, as well as the Science Museum and the Victoria and Albert Museum. Appropriately for an Elizabethan house, there were special collections of Elizabethan books, silver, furniture, armour, textiles and embroidery. There were paintings attributed to Gheeraerts, Hilliard, Dahl, Lely, De Wint, Prout and Etty. King George V's loan was a set of 'touchpieces', coins, bored with a hole, to be worn around the neck by those touched by a monarch for 'the King's Evil' - scrofula. Sir William Burrell, the millionaire Glasgow shipowner, loaned four pieces of tapestry. The artist Frank Brangwyn donated a set of his drawings of the Stations of the Cross. Paul Nash loaned one of his water colours. The National Art Collections Fund presented drawings by George du Maurier, the *Punch* artist and author of *Trilby*. Highlight exhibits included an Armada medal, Robert Dudley's fiddle, Bow and Chelsea porcelain and a Wedgwood toilet set. One room of the museum was devoted to Barking itself. Exhibits included archaeological finds, such as a funerary ring belonging to an Abbess, a medieval rent roll, election broadsheets, a constable's truncheon and items relating to the fishing trade - already referred to in the exhibition catalogue as a "forgotten industry."

The People's War

EVACUATION

Barking, with a particularly large school-age population located near a dense concentration of industrial premises and public utilities, all within a few miles of the centre of the capital, represented a high-risk target area for enemy action. Children from St Margaret's Church of England school were dispersed nationwide, to Welwyn Garden City, Northampton, Stoke-on-Trent, Burnley, Clitheroe and Maryport. Pupils of Gascoigne Road Junior School went to Somerset, while the children of Northbury School went to Bristol. Two hundred and fifty pupils of Barking Abbey School were relocated to Weston-super-Mare. The school buildings at Barking Abbey suffered severely from enemy action, being badly burned by bombing in June 1942. With the advent of flying bombs in 1944 a second wave of evacuees was despatched to Stafford, Chester, Leicester and York. Mothers who kept small children with them while they contributed to the war effort could take advantage of nurseries established at Eastbury House and Lodge Farm House in 1942.

THE ARP

Barking's unit of Air Raid Precautions (ARP) was based at Eastbury House and also occupied Eastbury School. A photograph taken in the grounds of Eastbury shows twenty uniformed Wardens, three of them female. Wally Blanchard, who joined the Royal Navy in 1942, had enlisted in the ARP in 1938 at fourteen. In anticipation of gas warfare Barking Council's decontamination unit began training in June 1939. Gas Cleansing Stations were organised at Park Hall, Axe Street, at 6 Woodward Road, at Eastbury School and at South East Essex Technical College. Rest Centres were established at Westbury School, the Church of England school in Back Lane, Dorothy Barley School in Harrold Road and Erkenwald School in Marlborough Road. A light rescue and ambulance service was operated from a Civil Defence depot at Cambell School, with women volunteers usually acting as drivers. There were First Aid posts in Broadway, Porters Avenue and

145. Evacuees from Gascoigne Road School.

146 and 147. ARP units during World War II. The above were stationed at Eastbury House, those below were at Creekmouth.

148. Civil Defence vehicles stationed at Cambell School in Langley Crescent.

149. A Home Guard exercise on the river.

at Barking Hospital. War Damage claims and salvaged furniture were dealt with at Central Hall, East Street. Conveniently consolidated at Ripple Road were the offices of the local Billeting Officer, the WVS, the Public Assistance Officer, who administered the Personal Injuries (Civilian) Scheme and handled 'Immediate Aid for the Homeless' – and the emergency mortuary in Castle School. Somewhat bizarrely the Refreshment Pavilion in Longbridge Road was to serve as a secondary facility in the event of particularly severe fatalities.

Work began on digging shelters in Vicarage Field in June 1939. Two hundred feet long, they were only 6' 6" high and 5' 6" wide. Their remains were unearthed in 1988 during the building of the new shopping precinct.

Barking's Home Guard detachment had its headquarters in Movers Lane and an anti-aircraft battery was stationed in Barking Park.

THE 'BATTLE OF BARKING CREEK'

The first time Spitfires ever fired their guns in anger was on 6 September 1939. Unfortunately, thanks to a technical fault on a radar screen, the target of the Spitfires of Hornchurch's No. 74 Squadron was six Hurricanes of No.56 Squadron from North Weald. Two of the Hurricanes were shot down. The pilot of one, Flying Officer Rose, managed to effect a landing, escaped unharmed and hitch-hiked back to base, still clad in the pyjamas in which he had been flying. His comrade was not so fortunate. Pilot Officer M L Hulton-Harrop, aged nineteen, was the first British airman to be killed in World War Two and is buried in the churchyard at North Weald.

Although the combatants may well have passed over Barking Creek, the actual dog-fight took place over the Medway. The misleading epithet became attached to the incident as it passed into RAF lore as a legendary example of the arbitrary foul-ups of war, Barking Creek being appropriated as a bathetic southern equivalent of music-hall references to Wigan Pier.

MORALE

A Forces House was set up in Vicarage Field to provide beds, meals and recreation to troops in passage. A mile of tramway track was taken up from London Road to be recycled as scrap. The Capitol Cinema gave a special matinee for local children who 'paid' their entrance with bundles of paper salvage.

During Warship Week in March 1942 Barking adopted the destroyer *Undaunted*, then building, and launched in July 1943. The ship took part in the bombardment of the Normandy beaches on D-Day. The following day, 7 June, it was diverted from another assigned bombarding position to pick up the Supreme Commander, General Eisenhower, and the Naval Commander of the Expeditionary Force, Admiral Ramsey, who had been visiting the beach landing-sites, and convey them back to Portsmouth so that they could report first-hand to the War Cabinet on the success of the invasion thus far. On leaving the ship Eisenhower presented it with his personal standard, autographed, which had flown from the ship's yardarm. *Undaunted* later saw action in the Adriatic and survived the war to be converted into an anti-submarine frigate. It remained in service until 1975.

Barking's biggest single contribution to national morale was surely 'Forces' Sweetheart' Vera Lynn,

150. *An advertisement for Handy Sauce.*

who was living locally when the war broke out.

A negative contribution was made by Barking-born Walter Purdy (1918-82), who qualified as a marine engineer and was a member of the Ilford branch of the British Union of Fascists. Taken prisoner after his ship was sunk off Narvik, as a POW Purdy met William Joyce (Lord Haw-Haw) and agreed to give propaganda broadcasts. He later served with the SS as a translator. After the war Purdy achieved the unwelcome distinction of being one of the four British citizens to be convicted of High Treason. His death sentence was commuted to life imprisonment and he was released in 1954.

And what of the inner man? The Ocean Preserving Company had no doubt of the value of its products to the battle on the Kitchen front - "From the beginning of the ... war the Ministry (of Food) realised the importance of Pickles, Sauces and Relishes as a valuable adjunct in providing a digestive value to monotonous and insipid foods, which have been so prevalent ...". In practice the company's efforts were constrained by a shortage of pickling vegetables, which in peace-time were normally imported from the Netherlands.

LOCAL HEROES

On 23 September 1940 John Duppa-Miller (1901-94), then a sub-lieutenant in the RNVR, assisted by Able-Seaman Stephen Tuckwell, RN, defused a huge magnetic mine which had fallen in the River Roding, near Barking Power Station. Magnetic mines contained a clock fuse timed to go off twenty seconds after impact. If the fuse failed to operate it could be re-started by any slight movement. As the amount of time which had run off before it had failed was an unknown quantity there might not be even twenty seconds to get clear ...

Barking's No 195
Combined Food Production Show

Promoted by the Barking Council, the Barking & District Allotment Holders' Society Ltd., the Barking Poultry and Rabbit Society, the Barking Red Cross Penny-a-Week Fund, and the Essex Council of Agriculture.

TO BE HELD IN THE

BATHS HALL,
EAST STREET, BARKING
on
Friday & Saturday, 27th & 28th August, 1943

OFFICIAL OPENING
by
HIS WORSHIP THE MAYOR OF BARKING
(Mr. Alderman A. G. Cook, J.P.)

On FRIDAY, 27th AUGUST, 1943, at 6.30 p.m.

Sir Charles Bressey, C.B., Chairman of the Essex Metropolitan Area Sub-Committee, British Red Cross Society will make an appeal on behalf of The Barking Red Cross Penny-a-Week Fund, to which fund the profits of the Show will be devoted.

151. Programme for a Food Production Show in August 1943.

If the ten-foot mine's ton of explosive had detonated, the local war effort would have been crippled by the blow to its energy supplies. Duppa-Miller and Tuckwell had to borrow a canoe from the Borough Engineer before they could even get to the mine. To quote a subsequent newspaper report:

"The mine could only be tackled at low water ... (and) ... lay at the exit of one of London's main sewers ... Had the clock started there would have been no chance of escape. The two men then tried to drag the mine onto a quay, but their ropes broke. Later they lifted it by a crane and made it safe."

On 14 January 1941 both men were personally invested by George VI with the newly-instituted George Cross for "great gallantry and undaunted devotion to duty." Duppa-Miller was later to defuse a parachute mine wedged beside the signal box at London Bridge station and at Coventry to lead a team which disabled fifteen mines. Before the war he had been Deputy Director of Education for Northamptonshire; he went on to become a Lieutenant-Commander and in 1951 published an account of his exploits *Saints and Parachutes*.

Aerial bombardment confronted Britain's beleaguered people with the reality of 'war on the doorstep'. Major A W Richards of Barking's Home Guard detachment was awarded the OBE for gallantry in two air raids. Cadet Barnes of the Air Training Corps' Barking Squadron received a letter of commendation from Air Marshal Mitchell

for breaking into a house to enable its occupants to escape after a blazing barrage balloon fell on it. Seventeen-year-old Cadet Norman Davies received the Cadet Gallantry Medal for administering first aid and rescue work during two air raids.

Other Barking heroes won their awards overseas. Bombardier G S Sharp, an old boy of Barking Abbey school, won the Military Medal with the Eighth Army in Italy. Operating Theatre Sister Gwen Owen, only daughter of the church-warden of St Margaret's, was also serving in Italy, aboard the hospital ship *Leinster*, dealing with casualties from the Anzio landings. Her coolness under air attack won her the MBE (Military Division). Nineteen-year-old Able-Seaman R A E Sida of Dawson Avenue was invested with the DSM for service on a destroyer escorting a vital convoy to besieged Malta. Another DSM was won by a former employee of the Chemical Supply Company in the course of the commando raid on St Nazaire.

THE INDUSTRIAL FRONT

As a major centre of manufacturing Barking made a significant and very varied contribution to the war effort. The Chemical Supply Company on Abbey Road, despite being bombed, worked day and night seven days a week to turn out the chemicals used in soldiers' portable 'tommy-cookers' and an anti-mosquito compound used by troops sweating their way through the jungles of south-east Asia. Barking Garage and Engineering Company produced two hundred mobile canteens, an invaluable source of comfort for rescue workers in blitzed-out areas. (A Barking Salvation Army man, Bandsman Harvey, actually manned a mobile canteen just behind the advancing front line after D-Day.) At the Harts Lane factory of Thames Plywood Manufacturers Ltd output was geared to front-line needs for pontoons, assault craft, motor torpedo boats and the versatile all-wood Mosquito aircraft. At Barking Creek massive concrete components, two hundred feet long and sixty feet high, were made for the artificial Mulberry harbours which provided logistic support for the Normandy landings. Troops transported on the *Queen Mary* might have felt that little bit safer for having the latest in light-weight life-jackets, manufactured by Fosbery & Co. of Barking. Fire risks on the *Queen Mary* had already been diminished by insulation produced by the Cape Asbestos Company of Barking, which, in wartime, concentrated on the production of explosives. Steel drums, needed by the thousand, were another key Barking product.

WORKING WOMEN

The systematic mobilisation of women for industry made a major contribution to victory. At Beckton they were employed as stokers and bricklayers' mates. Other women left the area to serve in the Women's Land Army.

Working hours in Barking's many factories were long but at least provided some distraction from worrying about loved ones far away. A peacetime hairdresser, engaged on making assault barges, remembered how, even above the noise of the machinery, a sudden silence could be detected when a name was called over the public address system and the individual concerned went to the main gate to receive a telegram, invariably informing them that a husband or son had been killed in action or taken prisoner. Working close to that same woman was a man whose only son went down with the *Hood*. He soldiered stoically on until one day when the radio, relayed over the PA system, played *God send you back to me*, then wept openly – and carried on.

BLITZED!

During the course of the war Barking's inhabitants were hit by twenty rockets, twenty-eight mines, thirty-eight flying bombs, two hundred anti-personnel bombs, over five hundred high explosive bombs and uncounted thousands of incendiaries. Barking's fatalities amounted to 236 plus 594 serious casualties and 1,891 lighter ones. Of local properties 638 were entirely demolished, 6,835 badly damaged and a further 11,747 lightly damaged.

The German raid on 7 September1940, which initiated the Blitz on London, caused major damage at Beckton gas works leading to serious interruptions of supply throughout the East End. Warne's rubber works also suffered heavy damage from a raid that same month.

Towards the end of the conflict Barking suffered heavily again from Hitler's 'revenge weapons – first the flying bombs (V1s), and then rockets (V2s), both unmanned. By September 1944, after eighty days of assault, 36 had fallen on the borough. Fifteen fell harmlessly in marshes or open country but the 21 that landed in built-up areas killed 43 people and injured 460 more, as well as damaging thousands of houses. Part of the terror was its arbitrariness. Seven were killed at Creekmouth and six in Mayesbrook Park while a V1, falling in St Ann's Road damaged fifteen hundred houses but caused not a single fatality. Although only 122 houses had been destroyed

152. *Part of a bomb damage report for Eastbury House. The damage affected the leaded lights of the front door.*

outright and another 497 rendered uninhabitable, 10,500, representing 60% of total housing stock, had been damaged. Eight hundred workers were employed in clear-up operations.

Then came the V2s. On 14 January 1945 a V2 gutted St Paul's church and severely damaged the Ministry of Labour, killing eight and injuring over two hundred. On the evening of the same day another rocket killed fourteen in London Road.

Considering Barking's remarkable concentration of industries dealing with potentially explosive or toxic substances, its labour force might have been forgiven for being even more apprehensive than the average industrial worker exposed to the attentions of the Luftwaffe. Yet there was no single incident comparable to the catastrophic Silvertown explosion of World War One.

A booklet parading the *Industries of Barking*, published by Barking Borough Council in 1948, took a surprisingly upbeat view of the wartime ordeal:

"In spite of its geographical situation, Barking did not suffer from bombing etc. to the extent of other Thames-side Boroughs. A high proportion of the bombs dropped conveniently in the Marshes, where they did no damage. Industrial production was affected very little through war damage, although one important exception was the Gas Light and Coke Company's works at Beckton. However, this is now all in the past ...".

The New Jerusalem?

The immediate post-war years of austerity were brightened by hopes of a better future, a just recompense for the sacrifices of wartime. Barking's Labour administration strongly reflected the aspirations of the Attlee government. Half a century later the extent to which their hopes have been fulfilled remains questionable.

HOUSING

The cessation of house-building in war-time, coupled with the damage caused by bombing, worsened still further the long-standing problem posed by sub-standard housing in Barking dating from late Victorian times. Many families still lacked access to the most basic of facilities. At the end of World War Two 3,400 houses in Barking were still without a bathroom. A few desperate souls sought their remedy in self-help. In the summer of 1946 98 families of squatters, consisting of 207 adults and 99 children, took over three former gunsite camps and two hutted camps. A third of the families were locals who had already put in applications for rehousing. As it was anticipated that the occupants would be *in situ* for at least two years before they could be offered alternative accommodation the borough pragmatically took over the management of these locations and installed gas, water and electricity supplies. Barking also erected 285 temporary homes, many of them along the Ripple Road, and between 1945 and 1954 built a further 66 to replace those destroyed by enemy action and 1,098 new ones, against a mere 146 put up by private builders.

Between 1954 and 1960 Barking then created the largest single housing estate built by a Greater London borough since 1945. The Thames View estate of 2,112 dwellings was built on reclaimed marshland. Some of the blocks of flats were nine storeys high. As a result Eastbury, formerly the smallest in terms of population of the borough's eight wards, became the largest. Despite the lessons of the Becontree experience in pointing up the problems arising from under-provision of the basic institutions of communal life and sociability Thames View was provided with a clinic and a library only in 1960, as the project was nearing completion, not at the outset, when such facilities, even if initially under-used, could have

153. *Ripple Road in the late 1940s. This section of the road, east of Lodge Avenue, has been transformed in the last forty years into a fast, ugly, multi-lane highway. Here, it is double-lane beside Castle Green. Pre-fabs, the temporary (but long-lasting) answer to the housing shortage, may be seen to its left.*

154. A room on the Mayesbrook Estate, 1948.

estate itself is isolated, the community fragmented, with little access to communal facilities. Services are basic, educational attainment poor, life chances limited." Alcohol dependency among the mothers of pre-school children was identified as a significant problem. Not at all what had been hoped for in the aftermath of victory ...

HEALTH

In 1946 Barking's, sometimes fiery, Medical Officer of Health, C Leonard Williams, published his annual report as a paperbacked, illustrated pamphlet of sixty-four pages in the hope that it would reach a wider public than "a small number of technical people" and thus become "a force in developing health consciousness." References to 711 local cases of scabies, and programmes for remedial action against squint, impart an initially Dickensian impression to the report but in fact the document is a testament to a progressive, pro-active health team that the borough could be proud of. It also makes clear that health workers were battling against severe shortages of personnel and resources in pinched, post-war Britain –

made a useful contribution towards building a sense of community.

Forty years later the Thames View estate was characterised by health professionals as "an area of high need, which has suffered from a history of low investment in services and amenities. The

155. Construction of the Longbridge Road Estate in 1949, showing houses in progress in Stratton Drive.

156. Outlying Barking – construction of the Thames View Estate 1957..

157. Central Barking – construction of The Lintons estate.

158. A quintessential late 1940s posed photograph, showing Barking's health service at work. A health visitor, in bonnet and uniform, talks to a cheerful mother who is blessed by the desirable quota of two children, with the elder one a boy.

a nationwide shortage of dentists, outworn hospital buildings and routine delays in securing admissions. The impact of shortages on the welfare of the population was also clear in ways which varied from undernourishment in women to the hazard of introducing bed bugs into newly-built homes because only second-hand furniture was available. The report began with a far-sighted warning that the community would be faced with the challenge of providing for the needs of an ageing population, which would have wide-ranging implications, not only for healthcare but also for housing. Noting that school assessments tended to put the "mental development" of Barking children at least a year *ahead* of comparable children from the East End by the age of ten, Dr Williams attributed this to better housing conditions and their consequent effect on children's sleeping. On the other hand, although the take-up of cod-liver oil, orange juice and vitamin tablets was higher in Barking than in other neighbouring boroughs, the MoH thought it was still too low and, if substantially improved, might have a significant impact on the incidence of premature births, which accounted for two-thirds of local

infant mortality. One obstacle to this which he identified was the current clumsy procedure of requiring that these supplements should be paid for with postage stamps, rather than cash. Dr. Williams was also particularly critical of the damage done by ill-fitting but fashionable shoes and the health hazards of dirty dustbins. He later achieved notoriety in the national press (and justification for some schoolboys) for advocating that people should wash less because soap diminished the natural oils which helped to preserve their health. The general tone of his Report, however, blends compassion, common sense and paternalism, informing the reader about what local health services have done, what they might do in future and what readers might do to help themselves and their families.

MARKING TIME?

The Barking Industrial Exhibition of 1950 aimed to show that, despite the persistence of shortages, the borough was back to 'business as usual'. But there was also abundant evidence that Barking was still lagging behind its more prosperous neighbour to the north. In 1950 the number of retail establishments per thousand inhabitants was 6.4 in Barking, 8.1 in Ilford. In 1949-50 total shop sales per head of population were a £109 in Ilford, £73 in Barking. The percentage living more than two to a room in Barking was 2.3, in Ilford 0.8. The percentage of 15- to 19-year-olds in full-time education in Ilford was 22, in Barking 8. The percentage of boys aged 17-19 in full-time education was 13 in Ilford, in Barking 3. National comparisons were no more reassuring than local ones. In 1951 the national average of population in the two highest of five occupational strata (professional and intermediate) was 18.3%; in Barking it was 8.7%. The percentage in the two lowest strata (partly skilled and unskilled) was 29.0, in Barking 35.4.

Over the next twenty years Barking's population was to contract substantially as a result of out-migration and a falling local birth-rate – from a 1951 peak of 78,170 to 65,035 by 1971 – scarcely a vote of confidence in the community's future. The local population was also undoubtedly ageing, compared with the youthful profile of the 1930s, although it was becoming middle-aged rather than elderly as yet. The percentage of residents above pensionable age was still below the national average. Some 89% of the population was classified as working-class. Half the local labour force worked within the borough at one of over a 150 local firms. One in six commuted into central London, as compared to one in four in Wanstead and Woodford. Most of the rest worked at Ford's in Dagenham, in the East End (in "the tangle of industries east of the Tower") or in West or East Ham.

The massive in-migration of the inter-war period had reshaped the composition of the local political elite decisively over the following decades. By 1962, of thirty Barking councillors and aldermen only six had actually been born in Barking, eight came from West Ham, nine from elsewhere in Greater London, three from South Wales and both party leaders from Warwickshire. The town's destiny was in the hands of a council totally dominated by Labour – 24 seats to six. The average age of councillors was fifty-two. Nine of them were female. Of the councillors twenty had had only an elementary education but 23 had undergone some kind of part-time further education. Eight had served as NCOs in the forces in wartime. The Labour majority formed a tight and assiduous coterie with an average of 24 years party service, roughly half of that period as councillors. Not only did each usually attend an average of over a hundred committee meetings a year, as well as party meetings and meetings with council officials, almost all served additionally as school governors and on the committees of voluntary bodies, clubs or trade unions. Six were JPs as well.

The 'New Jerusalem', 'cradle to grave' vision of the Labour government elected in 1945 became institutionalised in Barking as a local time-warp. The headings of a 1960s 'Official Guide' provide innocent testimony of the Borough Council's paternalistic ideals and objectives. The importance attached to children, health, welfare and the disadvantaged is attested by an impressively lengthy list of departments, agencies and programmes - Adolescents, Adoption, Blind and Partially-Sighted Persons, Chest Clinics, Child Care Officers, Child Guidance Clinic, Child Minders, Children's Homes, Chiropody, Day Nurseries, Deaf and Hard of Hearing, Dental Clinics, Disabled Persons – Occupation Centres and Sheltered Workshops, Domestic Help Service, Family Case-Work ("for families in fear of eviction"), Family Planning, Foot Clinics, Foster Homes, Handicapped Persons, Health Visitors, Homeless Persons, Home Nursing Services, Homes for the Aged and Handicapped, Hygiene, Immunisation, Laundry Service for the Incontinent, Marriage Guidance, Maternity Services,

Mental Health ("on call at all times of the day and night"), Midwives, Pupil Maintenance Grants (for children staying on at school after fifteen), Playleader Scheme, Unmarried Mothers, Vaccination and Wheelchairs, Loan of. A new level of affluence is attested by a heading for Abandoned Cars, the shadow of the past by others for Scabies and Tuberculosis. Cultural enrichment was represented by a local Arts Council and a Film Society Co-Operative. The library service not only loaned (free) "gramophone records, including speech and language instruction records" but also reproductions of Old Master paintings – three months, one per household. The Parks department provided facilities for rowing, sailing, bowls, cricket, netball, football, miniature golf, hockey, hurling, rugby, athletics, tennis and swimming. There was also a miniature railway.

It is a reminder of the discretionary power then possessed by local councils with the will to exert it that the borough could give financial assistance towards the cost of boarding education or for school clothing, meals and travel and even advances for house purchase and home improvements. It was also "prepared to accept loans from the general public for financing the Council's capital expenditure". In an age of privatisation, competitive tendering and contracting out it is salutary to recall that the Council catering service was "equipped to undertake speciality banqueting and formal functional (sic) catering in its public halls" as well as outdoor catering "for sports or similar large scale events". The Borough restaurant was, however, to close in 1982, more a casualty of changing lifestyles than of Thatcherism.

By the 1980s increased car-ownership in the borough meant the employment of a full-time road safety officer and 'energy awareness' meant that grants were available for home insulation. Changing leisure tastes were represented by the provision of squash courts, aikido instruction and a fitness room. 'Environment' had become a prominent and recurrent term in the Borough Guide. But there were still 3,000 applicants on the housing waiting list and 125 new applications a month. The new preoccupations of the 1990s included programmes to tackle drug abuse and to support single mothers, bottle banks for recycling and ombudsmen to deal with complaints against failures of public service provision.

THE ECONOMIC BASE

Sir Patrick Abercrombie's 1944 Greater London Plan envisaged that Barking would play a major part in the industrial reconstruction of the capital:

"Displaced industry would find suitable alternative sites adjoining the Creek ... or more likely on the industrial estate east of River Road. Several hundred acres (including present allotments, which it is assumed will ultimately be used for industry) are available ... and served by development roads; a siding is also available. This Barking industrial estate will form one of the principal areas for decanting industry from East London, as it is near the large LCC housing estate ... with its huge labour pool, much of which now travels to Central London for work. Industrial development here is, in part at any rate, of the heavier type ... such as engineering, concrete products and a wide variety of building materials, chemicals, timber and joinery etc.; it should be reserved for firms from the congested East End."

Barking's economic base in the 1960s was still characterised by industries which spanned a broad range – asbestos and aluminium, rubber and chemicals, gramophones, tape recorders and industrial clothing, power generation, paints, pharmaceuticals, packaging, plastics, plywood and piccalilli. But established businesses had already begun haemmorhaging away. Henderson's sliding-door factory relocated to Harold Wood in 1954. The Abbey Match Works closed in 1957, the Lawes Chemical Company in 1969, R White & Sons lemonade factory in 1972, Beckton Gas Works in 1976 and the Ford assembly line at Dagenham in 2002. The future was represented by the opening of a freightliner terminal south of Ripple Road in 1972.

By the end of the century there would still be a substantial presence for such locally traditional sectors as chemicals, engineering, construction, building materials and flooring. There was still even a sailmaker – an echo of the glory days of the Short Blue fleet. But, apart from printing and photography, most new businesses were geared increasingly to the provision of specialised services, ranging from shipping and security to waste disposal, container transport and industrial training courses.

THE CHANGING SCENE

Remnants of the old town continued to fall victim to the demolition crew. North Street police station went in 1955, The Barge Aground public house in 1973. The last trolleybuses went out of

159. *The new Barking Town Hall. Its pre-war style, inspired by Stockholm Town Hall, is due to the fact that it was designed in competition in 1936, but not actually completed until 1958.*

service in 1959. In 1986 East Street swimming baths were demolished and in 1988 Barking Park open air pool was closed. Compensation came in the shape of the Abbey Sports Centre in Axe Street, opened in 1986.

Contemporaries would, however, probably have been more aware of what was new. Long delayed by the war and post-war austerities, Barking's imposing Town Hall was finally opened in 1958. 1961 witnessed the opening of Barking Assembly Hall (now Broadway Theatre) and a new Station booking hall, which won plaudits from hard-to-please architectural critic Ian Nairn:

"one of the noblest new buildings in London ... It draws you in, where most stations repel ... wonderfully free from arty affectation, the perfect building to represent a modernized railway system. ... For the first time in a hundred years, the centre of Barking has been given a chance."

At a civic and institutional level the trend seemed still to be onwards and upwards. In 1962 South East Essex Technical College was designated a Regional College of Technology. In 1964 Eastbury House was at long last refurbished. In 1965 Barking and Dagenham were merged to

160. *Barking Railway Station in 1959, not long before its demolition.*

161. *Boating on the lake at Mayesbrook Park.*

create a single new London Borough. In 1966 the Central Library organised an exhibition to mark the 1300th anniversary of the foundation of Barking Abbey – the same library burned down in 1967 but reopened in new premises in 1974. Over a quarter of a century after the disastrous Thames floods of 1953 rendered fifty Barking residents homeless work began on the construction of a Barking flood barrier which was completed in 1983.

In 1968-70 mergers of three local colleges created the North East London Polytechnic, which in 1992 became the University of East London. A decade later, however, the University announced its intention to dispose of its Longbridge Road site by 2005 and concentrate its activities at its new Docklands campus.

As if in acknowledgment of the rapidity of redevelopment in 1975 a conservation area was established around the Abbey ruins. A decade later extensive excavations of the site were undertaken by a team from the Passmore Edwards Museum. As if making a nod to a fondly remembered East End tradition Barking Market was reopened in 1992. Vicarage Field shopping centre, by contrast, represented the contemporary face of consumerism.

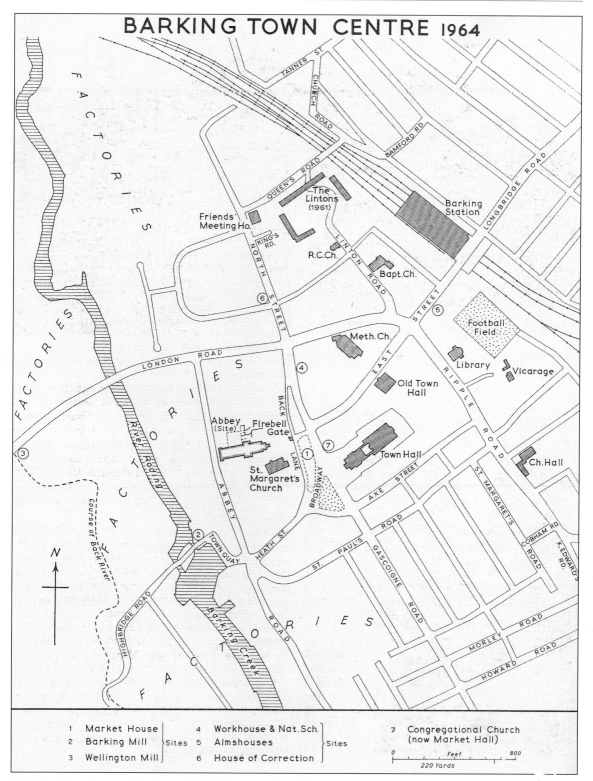

BARKING TOWN CENTRE 1964

1	Market House	
2	Barking Mill	}Sites
3	Wellington Mill	
4	Workhouse & Nat. Sch.	
5	Almshouses	}Sites
6	House of Correction	
7	Congregational Church (now Market Hall)	

162. *The Town Centre of Barking in 1964. (Map reproduced from the Victoria County History of Essex, Vol. V.)*

163. *Destruction of the old Central Library in Ripple Road by fire in 1967.*

164. *The new Central Library in 1974.*

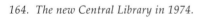

165. *Barking Market in the 1950s, an open market located near the Town Hall, between East Street and Axe Street. It was closed when the centre of Barking was redeveloped.*

AN URBAN RENAISSANCE?

The town centre of post-war Barking may have assumed the outward look of a reassuring modernity but the social fabric of the community failed to match its superficial air of well-being. At the turn of the millennium Abbey and Gascoigne wards, at the very heart of the town, were ranked among the 10% most deprived in England. In 1999 the Social Services department was listed by the government as one of seventeen failing so badly as to be placed on its special 'at risk' register. The local health authority was ranked 79th in the country. Local mortality rates were above the national average with deaths from lung cancer and coronary heart disease a particular cause for concern. The number of school exclusions stood at double the national average. Barking was also at the top of the national league for teenage pregnancies and with some 30% of its adult population divorced or separated almost ranked as a national marital disaster area. Although the Friends Meeting House had become a Sikh gurdwara as long ago as 1971 the increasingly multi-ethnic character of the local community only began to be seriously addressed in terms of council policy some thirty years later as a comprehensive range of guidelines,

targets and timetables was belatedly put in place. By then some 15% of the population was estimated to be from an ethnic minority background, including some 3,500 to 5,000 refugees and asylum-seekers. The preoccupations of local residents were reflected in the pages of *Citizen*, the monthly community magazine slickly produced by the borough's Public Relations department – 'Tips to protect your shed from burglars' and 'Hints to stop bogus callers'. Recurrent trumpeting of improved school examination results and sporting triumphs was matched in its pages by recurrent references to offensive phone calls, dodgy car dealers, truancy and domestic abuse.

Barking could, at least, claim to be the last place in the metropolitan area where a person earning less than thirty thousand pounds a year could still afford to buy a house. The average price of a property in the borough was £90,786, compared to £110,227 in Newham and £153,226 in Redbridge. The average for Greater London as a whole was £205,831. Unfortunately the average household income in Barking was only £19,124, placing the borough in this respect just ahead of Rotherham and Walsall, just behind Plymouth and Sunderland. One of the Borough's own strategy papers admitted candidly that Barking was

166. Gascoigne Road shown on a 1937 postcard. Note the poster advertising Masters matches, a local firm.

167. Construction of the Gascoigne Estate.

'not a typical London Borough. It has been re- markably homogeneous socio-economically and in terms of housing stock. A high proportion of the population have lived all or most of their lives in the Borough and migration is very low ... Average incomes are the lowest in the capital ... skills remain low, particularly among adults." Barking also had the lowest absolute number of inhabitants with graduate qualifications in all England - whereas over a third of the labour force of central London was of graduate status or its professional equivalent. The fact that film com- panies had also recently employed Barking lo- cations to replicate pre-Glasnost eastern Europe and Hitler's besieged bunker added little further encouragement.

In formulating a regeneration strategy borough planners placed major emphasis on the 'Thames Gateway' concept, contextualising Barking as a key component and potential beneficiary of new inward investment thanks to its proximity to Docklands and the excellence of its road, rail and underground services. Much optimism was also focused on plans to develop Barking Reach – two and a half miles of riverfront, jointly owned by National Power and the London Borough of

168. (*Left*) *Old houses in Axe Street.*

169. (*Below*) *Demolition of Axe Street.*

170. (*Above*) *A float in the Barking Carnival of 1965.*

171. *An aerial view of redevelopment around Barking Broadway in July 1972. The Barge Aground pub, demolished in 1973, can be seen on its old site before moving across the road. The car park in front of the Curfew Tower marks the site of the Elizabethan Market House demolished in 1923, and the old market place. At the bottom is R White's mineral water factory, demolished in the winter of 1972/3. It was built on the site of Bifrons House.*

Barking and Dagenham, which was identified as feasibly the largest site for housing development in the entire capital. Mindful at last of the lessons of Becontree and Thames View, planners envisaged not only the building of some 5,000 homes for some 15,000 future inhabitants but also the creation of 5,000 jobs and the provision of a full range of commercial and recreational facilities. It is not, however, immediately apparent that the realisation of such a vision would necessarily create a backwash of economic activity which would inevitably regenerate the hinterland as well. If planning for an 'urban renaissance' fails to tackle the problems of the existing community, rather than attempting to reinvent the past without its more evident mistakes, it may simply demonstrate that Barking Reach will remain beyond Barking's grasp.

Chronology

666 St Erkenwald founds Barking Abbey
687 First recorded reference to Dagenham
692-3 Hodilred's charter
693 Death of St Erkenwald at Barking
c. 870 Danes destroy Barking Abbey
950 Edred grants land to Barking Abbey
1066 William I lives at Barking Abbey
1086 Abbey estates recorded in Domesday Book
1145 Abbess Adelicia founds leper hospital at Ilford
c. 1175-9 Market first recorded at Barking
1254 First known reference to a shop in Barking
1279 Barking Abbey visitation by the Bishop of London
c.1300 St Margaret's becomes a parish church
1321 Manor of Westbury first mentioned
1330 Barking Abbey acquires the Dagenham manor of Cockermouth
1370 Curfew Tower built
1376-7 Major flood damage at Barking
1400 Fire Bell Gate first mentioned
1436-41 Edward and Jasper Tudor educated at Barking Abbey
1447 Handtroft/Hamthrough bridge known to exist
1456 Barking Abbey Rental made
1460 Curfew Tower rebuilt
1539-41 Dissolution and demolition of Barking Abbey
1539-1630 Manor of Barking held by the Crown
1556 Hugh Lavercock martyred at Stratford
1556-72 Eastbury House built
1557 Clement Sysley buys the Eastbury estate
1567-68 Court/Market House built in the Market Place
1574 Celia Glasenbery hanged as a witch
1580 Elizabeth Hardinge hanged as a witch
1628 Charles I sells the Manor of Barking to Thomas Fanshawe
1642 Sir James Cambell bequeaths money for a Free School
1653 Barking mapped for Thomas Fanshawe
1662 Sir Thomas Fanshawe bequeaths Market House and tolls to the benefit of Barking's poor
1672 Quaker burial ground established
1717 Manor of Barking passes to the Humfreys family
1719 Gunpowder magazine built at Creekmouth
1722 Barking workhouse established
1724 Smart Lethieullier excavates Barking Abbey
1730 Henry Carey writes *The Song of Barking*
1734 Dick Turpin and the Gregory Gang raid Longbridge Farm
1737 Roding Navigation Act improves river access to Ilford
1739 Press gang provokes the 'Battle of Creekmouth' with Barking fishermen
1762 Marriage of Captain James Cook to Miss Elizabeth Batts at St Margaret's

1764 Short Blue Fleet established
       Major floods
1783 John Wesley visits Barking
1786 Barking Workhouse Act
1787-8 Workhouse built
1791-2 New House of Correction built to the designs of John Johnson
1794 St Margaret's vicarage built
1801 Population 1,865
1803 Barking raises a volunteer corps of infantry
1807-10 Barking Road laid out to connect Barking with Canning Town
1810-12 New road built through Barking to connect London and Tilbury
       Building of West (Back River) bridge, Middle (Roding) Bridge and East (Hawkins) Bridge. Hamthrough Bridge over Back River demolished
1811 Merino sheep pastured at Bifrons
1815 Wellington Mill built
1818 Savings Bank formed
1824 Major floods
1828 National School built
1830 St Mary's, Ilford becomes a separate ecclesiastical parish
       Quaker congregation dissolved
1836-7 Barking Gas Company established
1840 Metropolitan police authority extended to Barking
1842 North Street police station built
       Major restoration of St Margaret's parish church
1844 Strike of Barking fishermen
1845 Burial of Elizabeth Fry in Quaker burial ground at North Street
1848 Major floods
1851 Population 5,365
1851-2 Baptist chapel built in Queens Road
1853 First meeting of Local Board of Health
1854 London, Tilbury & Southend Railway opened
1855 Victoria Dock built
       Local Board of Health dissolved
1857 Factory built at Creekmouth to manufacture artificial fertilizer
1861 Population of Barking 5,591 in 1,162 inhabited houses
1861-2 Construction of Northern Outfall Sewer
1862 Samuel Hewett's fleet relocates to Gorleston
1863 Sixty Barking fishermen lost in a gale off the Dutch coast
1866 World's largest jute factory opened in Fisher Street (Abbey Road)
       Malthouse built for Randells & Co in Fisher Street
1867 Construction of Beckton Gas Works begins
       Roden Lodge destroyed by fire
1868 Barking protests to the Home Secretary against discharge of sewage in Barking Creek
1869 Roman Catholic church of SS Mary and Ethelburga dedicated
1870 Telegraph service reaches Barking
1872 Church of England National school built
1873 South Essex Waterworks Company supply

reaches Barking
Salvation Army branch opened
1874 Freak high tide
1875 Barking Fair suppressed
1878 *Princess Alice* disaster
1880 Royal Albert Dock opened
Barking Rovers FC founded
1881 Mission to Deep Sea Fishermen founded
1882 Local Board of Health re-established
1884 Vicarage Field football ground opened
Burial Board for Barking opened
1885 Barking Hospital originates as a tent for the
treatment of infectious disease
North-east Abbey gate demolished
1886 Rippleside Cemetery opened
Barking leads Essex in adopting the Public
Libraries Act
Jute factory closed
1888 Ilford and Chadwell Wards detached to form
the administrative parish of Ilford
Barking to Pitsea branch line completed via
Upminster and East Horndon
Major floods
Jute factory re-opens
1889 Barking station rebuilt
Barking Town School Board established
Barking Rovers move to Eastbury Field
Beckton Gas Workers strike
1891 Jute factory closes
Quaker meeting revived
1892 Gascoigne Board School opened
1893 Baptist Tabernacle, Linton Road begun
Infectious Diseases Hospital opens at Upney
Meadow
1894 Barking becomes an Urban District Council
Town Hall and library built in East Street
Patent Cork Co. destroyed by fire
1895 First meeting of Barking Urban District Council
Great Freeze
William Warne & Co. take over jute factory
premises
1897 Barking Pumping Station and water-tower built
Brewery Tap public house built
Barking UDC takes powers to establish an
electricity supply
Northbury Board School and Barking Castle
School, Rippleside opened
1898 Charles Haddon Spurgeon opens new
schoolrooms and vestry rooms at the rear of
Linton Road Baptist Tabernacle
Barking Co-operative Society absorbed by
Stratford Co-op
Barking Park opened
1899 Fatal explosion at Hewett's Barking works
Red Lion public house built
Local electricity supply available to homes
1901 Thomas Stevens consecrated Bishop of Barking
Fishing Smack public house rebuilt
Creekmouth School opened
Barking St John's Ambulance Brigade founded

1901-2 Smallpox epidemic
1902 District Line reaches Barking
1902-6 First council houses built
1903 Tram services to Ilford and Beckton inaugurated
1904 Westbury School, Ripple Road opened
London Road Roding Bridge opened
1904-5 Tram services to Loxford Bridge and the East
Ham boundary begin
1906 Jolly Fisherman public house built
1907 First Lady Health Visitor appointed
1908 Barking station rebuilt
Friends meeting house built
1908-10 Abbey Match Works in Abbey Road built by
Jonkoping & Vulcan
1909 Handley Page works established at Creekmouth
1909-10 Abbey Road built as an extension of Fisher
Street
1911-12 Excavation of Barking Abbey by Sir Alfred
Clapham, President of the Society of Antiquaries
1912 Barking Gas Company taken over by Gas Light
and Coke Co. of Beckton
Bus service to London opened
1913 Asbestos factory opened
1914 Job Drain wins VC at Le Cateau
1917 Explosion at Barking Chemical Works
1918 National Trust buys Eastbury House
Barking Council owns 313 dwellings
1919 J John Masters takes over Abbey Match Works
Barking Manufacturers' Association founded
Midwifery service established
1921 Population of Barking 35,523 in 6,762 inhabited
houses
Building of Becontree estate begins
1922 Quayside millhouse demolished
War memorial dedicated in Barking Park
Barking Abbey school opened
1923 Elizabethan Court/Market House demolished
Visit of King George V and Queen Mary
Barking and Dagenham Post founded
A F Bulgin radio factory opened
1924 Barking bus garage opened
Central Library, Ripple Road opened
1924-8 Barking by-pass built
1925 George V opens Barking Power House at
Creekmouth
1926 Wellington Mill demolished
1927 British Match Corporation Ltd acquires Abbey
Match Works
1928 Central Hall built
Major restoration of St Margaret's parish church
1929 Barking tramways leased to East Ham and Ilford
councils
1930-35 Barking section (9,000 houses) of Becontree
estate built
1931 Population 51,270 in 10,965 inhabited houses
Barking Charter pageant marks Barking's
achievement of Borough status
Open air swimming pool opened in Barking Park

Burtons' tailoring store built at the corner of Broadway and East Street
1932 Roman remains found at Ripple Road
Barking Hospital opened
District line extended to Upminster
1933 England *vs* Wales match at Barking Town Workingmen's Quoit Club (Wales won 162 to 120)
1934 Bifrons senior school opened
Barking linked in to main London sewerage system
Barking and District Historical Society formed
1935 Bridge Street demolished
Elizabethan market buildings, Back Lane demolished
Foundation of Barking and District Archaeological Society
Barking Museum opened in Eastbury House
1936 South East Essex Technical College opened
Cecil House, Northbury House and former Workhouse demolished
Metropolitan line service extended to Barking in peak hours
Fulks/Northbury House, North Street demolished
1936-40 Barking trams replaced by trolleybuses
1937 London Road extended to join Ripple Road
Manor (formerly Jenkins) Farm demolished
1938 New fire station opened in Alfred's Way.
Whiting Avenue built
Estimated population 76,790
1939 'The Battle of Barking Creek'
1940 Conversion of tramways to trolley buses completed
Beckton gas works heavily bombed
Magnetic mine defused in River Roding
1942 Barking adopts *HMS Undaunted*
1944-5 V-bomb attacks
1945 Central Hall destroyed by a V2
Barking becomes a Parliamentary Borough
1946 Squatters occupy former military facilities
1948 Town links with Witten, Germany inaugurated
1950 Barking Industrial Exhibition
1953 Flood makes fifty Barking residents homeless
1954-60 Thames View estate built
1955 North Street police station demolished
1957 Abbey Match Works closed
1958 Barking Town Hall opened
1959 Trolleybus service ends
1961 Population 72,293

Barking Assembly Hall (now Broadway Theatre) opened
Station booking hall opened
Linton Road council flats opened
1962 South East Essex Technical College designated a Regional College of Technology
Fenchurch Street – Southend line electrified
1964 Eastbury House refurbished
1965 Barking and Dagenham merged to create a single London Borough
Grant of Arms by the College of Heralds
1966 Central Library exhibition to mark 1300th anniversary of the foundation of Barking Abbey
1967 Central Library, Ripple Road burned down
Closure of Beckton Gas Works
1968 College mergers creates North East London Polytechnic
1969 Lawes Chemical Company liquidated
1971 Friends Meeting House becomes a Sik gurdwara
1972 Freightliner terminal opened in Ripple Road
1972-3 R White & Sons factory demolished
1973 The Barge Aground demolished
1974 Central Library reopened in new premises
1975 Abbey conservation area established
1976 Beckton Gas Works closed
1979-83 Barking flood barrier built
1979 Barking formally twinned with Witten
1982 Barking Borough Restaurant closed
1985-6 Passmore Edwards Museum excavates Barking Abbey ruins
1986 East Street swimming baths demolished
Abbey Sports Centre, Axe Street opened
1987 Full Metal Jacket filmed by Stanley Kubrick at Gallions Reach,
Beckton Gas Works
1988 Barking Park open air pool closed
1992 Barking market re-opened
University of East London created
1996 Excavations at Barking Abbey
2001 London Borough of Barking and Dagenham Heritage Strategy launched
War memorial rededicated in Barking Park
2002 Ford's Dagenham assembly line closed
East London Transit Scheme announced, to link Ilford, Barking and Dagenham Dock by bus by 2006
Queen Elizabeth II visits Eastbury House during her Jubilee tour

Further Reading

(BDLD = Barking and Dagenham Libraries Department)

Barking Borough Council: *Industries of Barking* (Kent Service Ltd 1948)

Barking and Dagenham Heritage Map (BDLD n.d.)

The Book of Barking (Fleetway Press 1931)

Tony Clifford: *Barking Pubs Past and Present* (BDLD 1995)

Tony Clifford, Kathryn Abnett and Peter Grisby: *On The Home Front: Barking and Dagenham in World War II* (BDLD 1990)

Tony Clifford, Kathryn Abnett and Mark Watson: *Residents and Visitors: Some Barking and Dagenham Personalities* (BDLD 1992)

Tony Clifford: *Barking and Dagenham Buildings Past and Present* (BDLD 1992)

Tony Clifford and Herbert Hope Lockwood: *Mr. Frogley's Barking: A First selection* (BDLD 2002)

J. Compton: *The Schools of Barking* (Barking Corporation 1932)

Corporation of Barking Museum: *Souvenir of Inaugural Loan Exhibition* (1935)

Susan Curtis, Jennifer Murphy and Mark Watson: *More Views of Old Barking and Dagenham* (BDLD 1991)

Gillian Gillespie: *Footprints in Time* (BDLD 1999)

Robert J. Harley: *Ilford and Barking Tramways* (Middleton Press 1995)

Alan Hill and Susan Curtis: *Recording the Past: A Selection of local history articles by James Howson* (BDLD 1996)

Dr Robert Home: *A Township Complete in Itself: A Planning History of the Becontree/Dagenham Estate* (BDLD & University of East London 1997)

James Howson: *A Brief History of Barking and Dagenham* (BDLD 1990)

Herbert Hope Lockwood: *Where Was The First Barking Abbey?* (Barking and District Historical Society 1986)

Herbert Hope Lockwood: *Barking 100 Years Ago* (The Author 1990)

Herbert Hope Lockwood: *A Happy Thought: The Story of Barking and District Historical Society 1934-1994* (The Author 1994)

London Survey Committee, Eleventh Monograph: *Eastbury House* (Survey of London 1917)

Patrick O'Driscoll: Talk given on Shadwell – London's Lost Fish Market

J G O'Leary: *The Book of Dagenham: A History* (Borough of Dagenham, 3rd edition 1964)

Public Relations Unit, London Borough of Barking and Dagenham: *D-Day Remembered* (BDLD 1994)

R B Pugh (ed.): *The Victoria County History of Essex Vol. V* (University of London Institute of Historical Research 1966)

Anthony M Rees and Trevor Smith: *Town Councillors: A Study of Barking* (The Acton Society Trust 1964)

Gavin Smith: The Archive Photograph Series: *Barking and Dagenham* (Chalford 1996)

C. Leonard Williams: *The Health of Barking 1946* (Borough of Barking 1947)

The London Journal, Pamela Sharpe: 'The Barking Ladies': Migrant Female Labour and the Abbey Jute Mill 1866-91, *Vol. 22 (1997)*

Websites

London Borough of Barking and Dagenham: www.barking-dagenham.gov.uk/

Barking and East Ham United FC: www3.btwebworld.com/ikas2000history.htm

This is Barking!: www.vladimir.demon.co.uk/historic.html

Genealogy: www.combs-families.org/combs/records/england/essex/barking.htm

www.eolfhs.rootsweb.com